GLORIOUS THINGS

Glorious Things

MY HYMNS FOR LIFE

Sally Magnusson

With best wishes,

Sally Magnusson.

 **continuum**
LONDON • NEW YORK

Continuum

The Tower Building, 11 York Road, London SE1 7NX
15 East 26th Street, New York, NY 10010
www.continuumbooks.com

© Sally Magnusson 2004

First published 2004

British Library Cataloguing in Publication Data
A catalogue record for this book is available from the British Library.

ISBN 0-8264-7417-9

Typeset in Postscript Caxton by Tony Lansbury, Tonbridge, Kent.
Printed and bound in Great Britain by Cromwell Press Ltd, Trowbridge, Wiltshire.

For Anna

ᨳᨩᨳ *Contents* ᨳᨩᨳ

⁂ *Acknowledgements* ⁂

I would like to thank Peter Kearney, of the Catholic Media Office, for providing information on "Lord, you have come to the sea-shore"; Þorgerður Ingólfsdóttir, founder and conductor of the Icelandic youth choir, Hamrahlíðarkórinn, who helped me to track down the sheet music for Hallgrímur Pétursson's hymns; my father Magnus Magnusson for unstinting help with the Icelandic translations; and my mother Mamie Baird for infecting me with her own love of hymns.

My thanks also to the authors of the books I have gratefully pilfered for background. Among these were Andrew Barr's two entertaining volumes, *Songs of Praise: The Nation's Favourite* (Lion, 2001) and *Songs of Praise: The Nation's Favourite Hymns* (Lion, 2002); *My Favourite Hymn*, compiled by Graham Ferguson Lacey (Robson Books, 1999), which provided useful glimpses of other people's hymn preferences; *Favourite Hymns: 2000 years of Magnificat*, by Marjorie Reeves and Jenyth Worsley (Continuum, 2001); *Your Favourite Songs of Praise*, a compilation by F. Colquhoun (Oxford University Press, 1987); and *The New Oxford Book of Christian Verse*, chosen and edited by Donald Davie (Oxford University Press, 1981). An especially delightful find was D. H. Lawrence's short essay, "Hymns in a Man's Life" in his *Assorted Articles* (Martin Secker, 1930).

The hymn "Chief of chiefs" can be found with other prayers and blessings translated from the Gaelic in *Praying with Highland Christians*, by G. R. D. McLean (Triangle, 1988); English versions of the two Icelandic hymns are available in *Hymns of the Passion*, by

Hallgrímur Pétursson (Reykjavík, 1978); and W. H. Auden has collected some of the best of George Herbert's work in *Selected poems of George Herbert* (Penguin, 1973).

I am also grateful to those who have given permission for copyright material to be included:

We cannot measure how you heal
Words: John L. Bell and Graham Maule
(c) 1989, WGRG, Iona Community, Glasgow
From the song book "Love from below" (Wild Goose Publications, 1989)

Great is thy faithfulness
Thomas O. Chisholm
© 1923 renewed 1951 Hope Publishing Company
Administered by Copycare *music@copycare*
Used by permission

Who can sound the depths of sorrow?
Graham Kendrick
© 1988 Make Way Music
International copyright secured. All rights reserved. Used by permission

All in the April evening
Used by permission of Robertson Publications, a part of Goodmusic Publishing, Tewkesbury, UK

Lord, You have come to the sea-shore (Pescador de Hombres)
Spanish text and music © 1979 Cesáreo Gabarain
English translation © 1987 by OCP Publications, USA. All rights reserved. Used with permission

Chief of chiefs
G. R. D. McLean
Used with permission of SPCK Books

❧ Introduction ❧

For anyone with an allegiance to literary craftsmanship as well as to God, is there anything more exasperating than being invited to give voice to a mediocre hymn? The banalities, the platitudes, the easy rhymes, the cloying meekness, the bad poetry rescued only by a good tune – it's enough to drive you to a silent order. At those times the American poet Robert Lowell's outburst in "Waking Early Sunday Morning" could be mine:

> *O Bible chopped and crucified*
> *in hymns we hear but do not read,*
> *none of the milder subtleties*
> *of grace or art will sweeten these*
> *stiff quatrains shovelled out four-square –*
> *they sing of peace, and preach despair;*
> *yet they gave darkness some control,*
> *and left a loophole for the soul.*

But wait. There *are* hymns, lots of them, in which both grace and art do reign and which leave a space considerably larger than a loophole for the soul. The English poet John Betjeman knew that. He once smilingly trounced a supercilious young television interviewer who was insisting that hymns were worthless doggerel. "Ah, I see what you mean", the Poet Laureate said mildly, and quoted this:

> *His dying crimson, like a robe*
> *Spreads o'er his body on the Tree;*
> *Then am I dead to all the globe,*
> *And all the globe is dead to me.*

The young man was silenced.

The verse is from "When I behold the wondrous cross" by Isaac Watts, a hymn which expresses both profound emotion and complex theology in a form which only the ignorant or the truly pretentious would deny is art. And Watts was not alone in his achievement. Far from being merely functional aids to worship, many hymns are things of lasting worth in themselves: glorious things, to quote the flamboyant John Newton. Among these are hymns of doubt and frailty as well as joy and optimism; hymns of quiet conviction and defiant hopefulness; hymns which belong to their culture but also reach out to the universal; hymns which, for all the tendency to back-of-the-envelope versifying, still manage to convey a whiff of the eternal.

In the course of selecting my own favourites, I was surprised to discover how important hymns have been in my life. I had not realised that I knew, or liked, so many. From childhood to adulthood, through the rituals of marriage, baptism and death, across the seasons and the festivals, even in aspects of my job, I see they have always been there. Some of these are great ones, and some decidedly not so great, but all are redolent – in that wonderful way unique to hymns – of time, and place, and faith's sometimes erratic journey through a life-time.

Hymns are a subject on which few people who have come into contact with them, even if only perfunctorily, seem to be neutral. "What's your favourite hymn, then?" I hazarded recently in the vague direction of my nearest colleagues in the BBC Scotland newsroom. Religious zeal is not normally much in evidence in this neck of the woods, but I can report that the question provoked our most animated debate since the penalty decision at Lyons which put Celtic out of the 2003 Champions' League. One journalist immediately plumped for "Soul of my Saviour", and quoted it word for word. Another tore her attention from the news running order to place a bid for "In the bleak mid-winter". The deputy editor delayed a trip to the studio to wonder, dewy-eyed, why nobody had mentioned "Lord of all hopefulness", which had been sung at his recent wedding. Meanwhile my co-presenter, reading rather more organised intent into the question than had been there, announced he had a number of favourites and would e-mail me his choices later – which, come to think of it, he never did. The point is that everyone was interested, all instantly foraging dreamily in their past for suggestions and each one of us genuinely baffled by the preferences of everyone else.

"You like *that* one?" expostulated our "Soul of my Saviour" man when I declared my fondness for a modern Spanish hymn we had both heard at a funeral. "But that's just sentimental fluff. I can't stand it."

"But I can," I retorted cheerfully. To which, as he readily conceded, there is no answer.

Other people's reasons for adoring a hymn often seem as bizarre and eccentric as our own are rational and obvious. From *My Favourite Hymn*, a book compiled by Graham Ferguson Lacey with contributions from a range of vaguely public figures, I discover that Cherie Blair likes "Amazing Grace" because it was sung at the fiftieth anniversary of NATO; that Prince Michael of Kent likes "For all the saints who from their labours rest" because as a child his doctor's name was Saint, and when the man's entire family arrived late for church one Sunday, they had to process embarrassingly to their seats just as this first line was being sung; and that Joanna Lumley likes "Immortal, invisible, God only wise" for the unassailable reason that any hymn which starts with the word "immortal" gets her vote. To all of which one can only say, "Really?"

I have no doubt this will be your own reaction to some of my choices; in fact, it would be downright strange if you were to embrace every favourite of mine with glad cries. Hymn-singing may be a communal activity, but hymns and psalms speak resolutely to, and for, the individual. So personal and quixotic are our preferences, so private the ground in which affection grows or loathing proliferates, that the wonder is not how often we might dispute each other's taste, but that we do actually hold so many of the same hymns in common respect. These tend to be the ones we dare to call "great", those hymns appreciated for their happy marriage of words and music and their ability to escape the limitations of culture and satisfy some shared hunger in us all.

The hymns with the strongest grip on our affections are frequently those we sang, or had sung to us, as children. There is a respected TV foreign correspondent who to this day regularly chants "I will make you fishers of men" to calm himself down when writing scripts to an imminent deadline. He says he can't get it out of his head. These childhood hymns go deep – so deep that although you may not consciously even have liked them, or been secretly afraid of the gory crucifixion images, or indeed, like my mother who can still recite by heart some of the most complex metrical psalms, not have understood a word at the time they were being learned, yet by the mysterious action of tune and word-picture on the porous mind of a child, they remain a part of you forever.

The writer D. H. Lawrence understood this. In his essay "Hymns in a Man's Life" he says the hymns which he learned as a child now mean "almost more" to him than the finest poetry, having long outlived his jettisoning of the Christianity which underpinned them. With endearing arrogance he notes: "Salvation, heaven, Virgin birth, miracles, even the Christian dogmas of right and wrong – one soon got them adjusted." Yet he remains "eternally grateful" for the religious teaching and the hymns, because they filled his childhood with wonder. He describes the effect of those hymns beautifully: "They live and glisten in the depths of the man's consciousness in undimmed wonder, because they have not been subjected to any criticism or analysis."

Mind you, this is only partially true. Childhood memories and a lifetime's familiarity do invest many hymns with a power they lose when inspected coolly on the page. But in making his breezy adjustments to the Christian cosmology, Lawrence denied himself the possibility of discovering that some of the hymns which have been surreptitiously furnishing our minds as we grow up work in precisely the opposite way: the wonder expands. Just as familiarity and a rousing tune can obscure all manner of vacuous sentiments, so they can also blind us to valuable insights and lovely poetry. In reviewing my own favourites, I have felt not only disappointment at how slight some appear when analysed cold, but also – and actually more often – exhilaration at how fresh and wise and beautiful are others I had never taken the trouble to ponder before. The joy of having your mind well furnished with hymns is in being able to enjoy both sorts: the exquisitely polished heirloom as much as the comfy old chair which, for all its faults, is simply too dear to throw out.

It is difficult, perhaps impossible, to separate your feelings for some hymns from the context in which you have sung them. Hymns can be as evocative as the perfume of a flower which assails you in a strange place on a summer's night, piercing your heart with the thought of balmy childhood evenings playing among a neighbour's shrubbery. You stand there transfixed, drunk with sweetness and memory, incapable of reacting in a detached way to this modest garden shrub with the unexceptional red blossom. In the same way Lawrence explained that he had long loved "O worship the Lord, in the beauty of holiness" because the first line had been painted in big letters over the organ-loft in the chapel he attended as a child; seeing it there invested the hymn with a kind of magic. He acknowledged that "gold of obedience and incense of lowliness" in the third line did not mean very much and that even the phrase "beauty of holiness" was suspect; but the verse still produced in him a sense of splendour. I, on the other hand, have no pale green organ-loft to help me overcome the conviction that "gold of obedience and incense of lowliness" is just plain bad.

This highlights a problem we all have in presenting hymn preferences to others. How, I wondered, was I was going to lead others through 35 idiosyncratic choices of mine without explaining about the organ-lofts in my own life? Could I take you with me on a rather bumpy ride through "Blessed assurance" without the company of my grand-mother? Could I include "Fight the good fight" without writing about the death of my brother? Could I entice you into one of the finest funeral hymns in any language without introducing you to my Icelandic heritage, along with the incomparable Hallgrímur Pétursson, the wife who was abducted by pirates and the little daughter who died too soon? Was there any other way to explain my affection for the hymn so bluntly trashed by my colleague as sentimental fluff than to tell you about Cardinal Thomas Winning?

The answer, I concluded, was no. If this has given the book more of an autobiographical flavour than I originally intended, I justify it with the hope that, in the best communal traditions of the hymn, my memo-ries and associations will have the effect of stimulating your own.

Inevitably I have also been guided by taste and (let's face it) preju-dice. Although "When I behold the wondrous cross" and "Soul of my Saviour" have succeeded in storming past my defences, I can nor-mally stand only so much blood-soaked imagery before lunch. Ropey grammar bothers me, too, which is why you will hunt in vain for John Newton's "Amazing Grace", the claims of which on my affection have been quite overwhelmed by the grammatical infelicity of the line, "We've no less days to sing God's praise". Why not leave that verse out, I hear you cry. Yes, but I'm afraid the rest of the hymn has been ruined for me by the mere thought of that line. You have to be comfortable with a hymn before you can offer it the emotional and intellectual assent which enables it to mediate a conversation with God – and unfortunately no one schooled as rigorously as I was in using the word "fewer" before a plural noun can be comfortable with "no less days". I know it sounds like a superficial judgement on a fine hymn, but to my ear the discord just drowns out everything else.

So where there is a choice between good poetry and sound theology, I find myself erring towards Lowell's "milder subtleties of grace or art". Other people's preference will be the other way around, and I understand why. Indeed no less a luminary than John Wesley agrees. In his preface to the 1780 *Collection of Hymns for the Use of the People called Methodists* Wesley praised the finest of these for "the purity, the strength, and the elegance of the English language", but argued that of infinitely more moment was the spirit of piety breathing through the book, which he hoped would encourage the devotion of the truly pious reader. What he doesn't mention is that plonking rhythms and lazy rhymes can drive the less intrepidly pious up the wall.

Nevertheless I have tried to remember that, while they are all literary vehicles, few hymns were written to be dissected on the page like a piece of T.S. Eliot. From the earliest Hebrew psalms to the latest guitar-twanged choruses, they have been composed as a means of worshipping God, of enabling believers to express communally in song what they might wish to say privately in prayer, but have not the art, nor always the heart, to do so.

The first Christian hymn is considered to be the Magnificat, the outpouring of joy and thanksgiving from Mary, expectant mother of Jesus, as recorded in the first chapter of St Luke's Gospel. Indeed you could argue that her ecstatic cry –

> *My soul doth magnify the Lord,*
> *And my spirit hath rejoiced in God my Saviour –*

has been the theme of just about every hymn worth its salt ever since (with the exception of a few, like Blake's "Jerusalem", which have sneaked into the pantheon on the strength of some blinding poetry and an immortal tune). Later St Paul encouraged early Christian congregations to sing psalms, hymns and spiritual songs. St Ambrose, fourth-century Bishop of Milan, is credited with introducing to church services the regular singing of hymns in Latin outside the liturgy of the mass. In the sixteenth-century Protestant reformers snatched hymn-singing from the exclusive clutch of clergy and choirs and gave the people metrical versions of the psalms to sing. It then took Isaac Watts in the eighteenth century, followed by the Methodist Wesley brothers, to begin the process of prising Nonconformist congregations away from Old Testament psalms to a fuller Christian celebration, with an emphasis on personal salvation. By the nineteenth century the Anglicans were getting in on the act. "Why should the Dissenters have all the best tunes?" was at least partly the thinking behind a veritable flood of Victorian hymn-writing. By the latter half of that century mass evangelical rallies were being moved to tears by the emotionalism of a new brand of gospel chorus, and social issues were starting to make their presence felt in compositions. Both those trends continued in the hymn-writing of the twentieth century, along with a new internationalism in the dissemination of hymns from across the world.

In each of these epochs, some hymns and psalms have shone brighter and spoken more personally to succeeding generations than others. Several are represented here, including one or two modern ones which have not had a chance to sit the test of time but which I think stand comparison with proven favourites. Contemporary hymns are often less sure at distilling difficult truths, but they tend to be good at communicating feelings, something which, even at its most glib, is an important function of a hymn. They are also adept at capturing the urgent, anxious, socially indignant, painfully honest kind of faith which is the hallmark of our own times. The best of them do it with considerable eloquence.

And then, of course, there is the music, the other half of the composition, the vessel which carries the words straight to the heart (or right over the head, as the case may be) and roots them in the memory. A reasonably good tune can inspire a stolid verse to unimagined heights of vivacity, whereas I fear only the greatest poetry (Psalm 121, for example) can expect to survive a dreary arrangement. Out of the often serendipitous process that brings words and music together, sometimes many years apart, it is frequently the music composed for a different purpose entirely – "Finlandia" by Sibelius, for instance, or the tune associated with the old Scots ballad "Ye banks and braes", or the traditional Irish air "Slane" – which really release the sacred words of a hymn to fly.

Over the years words and music have grown into single pearls, precious things whose value, either through familiarity, disdain or the decline of the Christian culture in which they flourished, we are increasingly in danger of not appreciating. They are the work of people across the centuries who had precious little in common – among them, in these pages alone, an Irish hermit, Gaelic farmer, Italian monk, Icelandic pastor, American journalist, Welsh preacher, Scottish printer, a king, a pope, a future cardinal, a ploughman and a former slave-trader – except an allegiance to Christ and a gift for communicating it. For centuries these hymns have been providing a voice for the dumb, a vocabulary for the inarticulate and a prayer when minds feel empty. They are a glorious heritage.

The poem to set against Robert Lowell's lines is George Herbert's "The Quidditie", written in the seventeenth century:

> *My God, a verse is not a crown,*
> *No point of honour, or gay suit,*
> *No hawk, or banquet, or renown,*
> *Nor a good sword, nor yet a lute:*
>
> *It cannot vault, or dance, or play;*
> *It never was in France or Spain;*
> *Nor can it entertain the day*
> *With my great stable or demain:*
>
> *It is no office, art, or news,*
> *Nor the Exchange, or busie Hall;*
> *But it is that which while I use*
> *I am with thee, and most take all.*

Perhaps the quiddity, or essence, of a hymn is just this: that while we are engaged in singing it, we are in some quite profound sense "with thee" – in communion with the God to whom we are together offering it. Wholeheartedly or tepidly, with lush instrumental backing or to the faltering accompaniment of some tinny organ, our minds devoutly on the words or wondering vaguely whether we remembered to lock the front door, in singing these hymns over the years with different people, in different places, at times significant and insignificant, we set in place without even knowing it the cornerstones of a life.

These are mine.

1. BY COOL SILOAM'S SHADY RILL

By cool Siloam's shady rill
How fair the lily grows!
How sweet the breath, beneath the hill,
Of Sharon's dewy rose!

Lo! such the child whose early feet
The paths of peace have trod,
Whose secret heart with influence sweet
Is upward drawn to God.

By cool Siloam's shady rill
The lily must decay;
The rose that blooms beneath the hill
Must shortly fade away.

And soon, too soon, the wintry hour
Of man's maturer age
Will shake the soul with sorrow's power
And stormy passion's rage.

O thou whose infant feet were found
Within thy Father's shrine,
Whose years, with changeless virtue crowned,
Were all alike divine,

Dependent on thy bounteous breath,
We seek thy grace alone,
In childhood, manhood, age, and death,
To keep us still thine own.

WORDS: Reginald Heber (1783–1826)
MUSIC: "Belmont" by William Gardiner, 1812

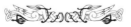

— 11 —

Reflections

If ever a hymn was able to infiltrate my affections, slipping past the radar which usually provides a reliable alert to incoming sentimentality, it is this one. Perhaps that is because I sang it five times with a downy-haired bundle in my own arms, at that hormonal stage of early motherhood when you burst into tears if you so much as spy a passing duckling. Or perhaps its potency begins much further back, when I was baptised to its incorrigibly sweet strains myself at Wardlawhill Church in the Scottish burgh of Rutherglen. Then, as now, the congregation would have found itself almost cooing the words, like a lullaby. In that sense it was my first hymn.

In all the times I sang it at the christenings of other people's children and eventually of my own, I had no idea that we were missing out Reginald Heber's original two middle verses. The Church of Scotland hymn book made no mention of decaying lily or fading rose, nor of the coming chill hour of maturity when the soul would shake with sorrow and storm with rage. No, in tiny Baldernock Church, in the parish north of Glasgow to which my family moved during my childhood, it was only the rose's sweet, newly budded breath which was permitted to waft over our babies.

As the infant was carried forward, more often than not offering an impressive early display of "stormy passion's rage", the congregation would rise to sing, bathing parents and child in the cooling tranquillity of Siloam's shady rill. Every mother in the place would gulp. Then, with the minister poised to provoke new paroxysms of fury by dripping water on the infant forehead, the final verse swept through the church, calm in its simplicity and finally comprehensive in its prayer for this baby's life "in childhood, manhood, age, and death". It never occurred to me that "manhood" was sexist. The sentiment was genuine, the grace all-inclusive and the love which enveloped the baby palpable.

For 25 years the musical accompaniment was provided by a retired cinema organist by the name of Lyndon Laird, who imported the uninhibited brio of the mighty Wurlitzer into that ancient country church every Sunday. Seated at the harmonium under the window, a tiny, wizened, Dickensian figure in long overcoat, brown scarf and black beret from which escaped wisps of white hair, he covered every hiatus in the service with melodies suspiciously reminiscent of a sing-along at the Odeon. The congregation practically waltzed to their seats to the tune of "Tiptoe through the tulips" and the minister was later blown out of the door with the help of "Wait till the sun shines, Nellie". Babies had the best of it, serenaded down the aisle to the soothing strains of "Toora-loora-loora, it's an Irish lullaby", before a deft change of key led the rest of us towards cool Siloam.

Reginald Heber wrote the hymn in 1812, while a vicar himself at Hodnet in Shropshire. Since he was remembered by parishioners for his merry sense of humour, I suspect he would have approved of our Mr Laird's blithe rendition.

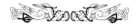

2. THE MAISTER CAME UP TO THE CITY

The Maister came up to the city,
His hert it was fu', unco sair.

He lookit aroun' him wi' pity
Nae ane in this world could share.
And aften he said, "I would gaither
Ye in frae the storm and the stress,
And be to ye a' as a saviour
Tae guide ye in tenderness.
Noo, bairnies, tak tent and receive.

My airms roun' ye a' I would weave.
List to my pleadin',
It's ransome you're needin'.
Come to me noo and believe."

Maister Master
hert heart *fu'* full *unco* very
sair sore
lookit looked *wi'* with
nae ane no one
aften often *gaither* gather
frae from
a' all
tae to
noo, bairnies now, children
tak tent pay heed
airms arms
pleadin' pleading
needin' needing
noo now

WORDS AND MUSIC: John Fulton Greig (1859–1916)

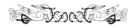

⚛ *Reflections* ⚛

John Fulton Greig, my great-grandfather, was a music compositor at the Glasgow printworks of Aird and Coghill, where his job was to set and correct type for the presses. It was a good job. My grandmother Sarah, who was born in 1886, second-eldest of his eight children, sailed through her childhood believing she would one day become a princess, since her father was the only man in their street who wore a gentlemanly hat to work, rather than a cap. Although that fantasy died abruptly when she started her first job as a French polisher in a furniture factory, John Greig was indeed a well educated, distinguished figure. He had a keen appetite for literature, and in his spare time composed verses of his own, two of which were published in a book of hymns.

My mother Mamie first sang this one to me years ago. She was telling me at the time about her grandfather's love of words. Suddenly, somewhat to her own surprise, she was singing his hymn, the one Sarah had taught her more than 50 years before and which she had barely sung since. The tune is an unpretentious melody, which she reckoned her grandfather had composed himself. But it was the words, in the supple vernacular of lowland Scotland, that entranced me.

Here is Jesus not as king but as father, addressing his children in the affectionate Scots diminutive as "bairnies", longing to weave his arms around them and keep them safe from life's storms. How much of Jesus the man is revealed in that deceptively understated line, "His hert it was fu'"; what reams of theology are compressed into those seven bald monosyllables, "Nae ane in this world could share". Here is the gospel, personal and intimate, from a man who, as a Sunday School superintendent at Glasgow's Barony Church, knew that the deepest mysteries of faith could still be grasped by a child. His hymn pares the gospel to its essence. "Come to me now," says the Master, "and believe."

I have not been able to track down the book of hymns in which this one appeared; it was probably published by John Greig's employers, Aird and Coghill. But the words here are exactly as my mother recalled them. I have no idea how widely it was known or how many people ever sang it. To escape the fetid atmosphere of industrial Glasgow, John Fulton Greig moved his family to the nearby royal burgh of Rutherglen, where he used to recite his poetry, along with other snippets of literature which had taken his fancy, at small social gatherings. I like to imagine him sitting down eagerly at the piano one evening in some draughty church hall and, with a twirl of his black moustache, teaching his audience the new hymn he had just composed.

I would love to hear it myself one day, sung by a congregation as he intended. The hymn deserves it.

John Fulton Greig, my great grandfather

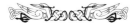

3. BLESSED ASSURANCE

Blessed assurance, Jesus is mine:
O what a foretaste of glory divine!
Heir of salvation, purchase of God;
Born of his Spirit, washed in his blood:

This is my story, this is my song,
Praising my Saviour all the day long.

Perfect submission, perfect delight,
Visions of rapture burst on my sight;
Angels descending bring from above
Echoes of mercy, whispers of love:

Perfect submission, all is at rest,
I in my Saviour am happy and blest –
Watching and waiting, looking above,
Filled with his goodness, lost in his love.

WORDS: Frances Jane van Alstyne (Fanny Crosby) (1820–1915)
MUSIC: Phoebe Palmer Knapp (1839–1908)

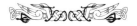

ᕱᕲᕳ *Reflections* ᕱᕲᕳ

This is a hymn which, you feel, just had to be written by someone called Fanny. Its blend of confidence, submission and angelic rapture, along with a breezy refusal to worry about using an identical rhyme twice, places its origin as firmly in the nineteenth century as its American writer's name. I like it because my grandmother used to sing it to me long ago. Take away her voice humming the chorus as she soothed one child after another to sleep and I'm not sure what I'm left with. But it doesn't matter. Fanny Crosby's artless song has taken root too deep in my memory and coiled itself too tightly around my heart to succumb at this late stage to textual analysis.

John Fulton Greig's daughter Sarah, my mother's mother, flitted quietly through my childhood, thin and bent from a lifetime's domestic labour bringing up first her younger siblings and then her own children in a succession of cramped tenements in Rutherglen. I remember my grandma as a small, frail figure in a dark cardigan, always buttoned up to the neck against the cold. My father used to call her Weeskin, an affectionate adaptation of the Icelandic *litla skinnið*, or "little skin". I remember how it felt to caress her cheeks, worn and sunken but infinitely soft to kiss. By the time she came to live with us in the 1960s her mind was wandering a little, but the cantankerousness of old age seemed to have passed her by. If it is true that our personalities are distilled into their essence in old age (something my own children may read with alarm), then hers was concentrated goodness.

"Blessed assurance" was her song. She patted her grandchildren to sleep with a chorus of "This is my story, this is my song", which none of us has ever forgotten. "Praising my Saviour all the day long," she would murmur. And in a sense she did.

The chorus has survived in my own household as a lullaby. For years I sang each of my brood to sleep at night with a ditty we called "Dum-bi-di-doo-doo", which you will see (if you can bear to check) matches the syllabic beat of "This is my story". Lovey-dovey words were then improvised in time to the rest of the tune, which is a gently soporific melody by Phoebe Knapp, an American friend of Mrs Crosby.

Thus has "Blessed assurance" lived on for me, debased and domesticated for sure, but retaining always a hint of the fragrance of my grandmother's personality and at least a whisper of that story which she and blind Fanny Crosby were happy to sing all the day long.

My grandmother, Sarah Greig

4. SILENT NIGHT

Silent night, holy night!
Sleeps the world; hid from sight,
Mary and Joseph in stable bare
Watch o'er the child beloved and fair,
*   Sleeping in heavenly rest.*

Silent night, holy night!
Shepherds first saw the light,
Heard resounding clear and long,
Far and near, the angel-song,
*   "Christ the redeemer is here!"*

Silent night, holy night!
Son of God, O how bright
Love is smiling from thy face!
Strikes for us now the hour of grace,
*   Saviour, since thou art born!*

WORDS: Joseph Mohr (1792–1848)
TRANSLATION: Stopford Augustus Brooke (1832–1916)
MUSIC: Franz Grüber (1787–1867)

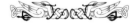

❧ *Reflections* ❧

M y father, Magnus Magnusson, is Icelandic. When he was only a few months old his family moved to Scotland, where his father became European export manager for the Icelandic Co-operative Society in the Edinburgh port of Leith. One of the delights of the traditions which my grandparents brought with them was that our family celebrated Christmas the evening before everyone else, as we still do. It began at 6pm on Christmas Eve, when the clan would gather at my aunt's house in Edinburgh for a candlelit meal, followed by carols around the tree and presents handed out with grave formality by my grandfather, Sigursteinn, resplendent in black dinner suit below a shock of white hair.

"Silent Night" was invariably the first carol to be sung, the hymn which inaugurated our Icelandic Christmas. We sang it together as we walked, hand in hand, around the invariably huge fir tree in the corner of the sitting room, first one way, then the other as a new verse began. The first time was always in Icelandic. It was mainly the adults who managed the words of "*Heims um ból*", we Scots-born children having failed to pick up much more of the language than *takk*, the word for "thankyou", an indispensable tool on a night like this. Then we sang the hymn in English.

Oh, but it was a magical experience, as the candles on the tree flickered and smoked against the black window, to sing of light and angel song and the striking of the hour of grace on a night long ago. Naturally, we children watched for the guttering of the last candle with an excitement which had rather more to do with the imminent striking of the hour of presents, but what made the evenings unforgettable were the play of light and darkness, the aroma of cigar smoke, the swish of long evening dresses around the tree and, above all, the soaring romance of that evocative carol.

While Icelanders inherited Christmas Eve from their one-time colonial masters, the Danes, Queen Victoria's husband Albert is credited with importing similarly romantic, child-centred festivities into Britain. "Stille Nacht", composed in Austria in the early nineteenth century, is the hymn which more than any other came to encapsulate this Germanic Christmas dream.

It is said that Joseph Mohr, an assistant priest at St Nicholas Church in Oberndorf, was inspired to write it by the starlit beauty of the mountains as he walked home. According to the story, the church organ broke down on Christmas Eve, 1818. Next morning Mohr's hymn was spontaneously set to music by the temporarily redundant organist, Franz Grüber, and sung to the accompaniment of a guitar.

By 1858 it was being translated into English. Today there are so many versions that it can be hard to remember whether we are enjoying a silent night with Mary and Joseph in stable bare or whether yon virgin is nursing a holy infant on a still night. But whatever the precise nativity details, the carol remains for many of us the essence of Christmas.

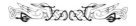

5. I TO THE HILLS WILL LIFT MINE EYES

(PSALM 121)

I to the hills will lift mine eyes,
*   from whence doth come mine aid.*
My safety cometh from the Lord,
*   who heaven and earth hath made.*
Thy foot he'll not let slide, nor will
*   he slumber that thee keeps.*
Behold, he that keeps Israel,
*   he slumbers not, nor sleeps.*

The Lord thee keeps, the Lord thy shade
*   on thy right hand doth stay:*
The moon by night thee shall not smite,
*   nor yet the sun by day.*
The Lord shall keep thy soul; he shall
*   preserve thee from all ill.*
Henceforth thy going out and in
*   God keep for ever will.*

WORDS: Scottish Psalter, 1650
MELODY: From Scottish Psalter, 1615

⊗⊗ *Reflections* ⊗⊗

The Sunday services I remember from my youth at Baldernock, in the lee of windy Craigmaddie Moor, normally began with the singing of a metrical psalm or paraphrase. Mr Laird's usual panache on the organ seemed to fail him at this point and the lack of musical decoration in the arrangements or even, as far as I could judge, any melody at all at times, meant that the opening hymns often exuded a dirge-like dreariness which drew many an eye to the window straight ahead of us. "I to the hills will lift mine eyes." And I did. Frequently.

There was no stained glass at Baldernock to divert mine eyes to artfully heavenly images; instead I could look straight through to the heavens themselves, the sky in its changing moods with the undulating green of the farm-lands below. Out there was the cemetery, where I could imagine the cattle thrusting their inquisitive muzzles over the hedge, the curlews curving past with their bubbling call. Hares would be lolloping over those fields, sparrow-hawks patrolling the hedgerows, cars braking fiercely on their way up the hill to avoid the tiny rabbits lurching timidly across the road.

Yes, those were hymns for day-dreaming. But, in truth, Psalm 121 was the one least likely to cause my attention to wander, because the poetry was so good. Those images of the protectiveness of God were arrestingly evocative: the Lord who made heaven and earth never slumbering on his watch, staying close as a shadow, preventing even a foot from sliding, keeping the soul safe.

My appreciation of the psalm was always in danger of ending in bathos when I reached "Henceforth thy going out and in", a point at which my mother had once confided her private vision of a troop of hens sallying forth. But it was rescued by the last line, the emphatic, dignified simplicity of "God keep for ever will".

When I hear the psalm sung today, to the stately (one of the better euphemisms for dreary) tune from the Scottish Psalter, I think of that old grey sandstone kirk with the gallery you climb to from outside, the belfry on the front wall, the watchhouse built to shelter volunteers who used to guard the churchyard from bodysnatchers in the dead of night. And I think of the people who have been gathering at that spot since monks laid the stones of the first church there more than seven centuries ago, generations of them, all lifting their eyes to the hills and every one of them helped to feel secure amid the slips and slides of life by the promise that God would keep them for ever.

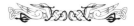

6. FIGHT THE GOOD FIGHT

Fight the good fight with all thy might;
Christ is thy strength, and Christ thy right;
Lay hold on life, and it shall be
Thy joy and crown eternally.

Run the straight race through God's good grace,
Lift up thine eyes and seek his face;
Life with its way before thee lies,
Christ is the path, and Christ the prize.

Cast care aside, lean on thy Guide;
His boundless mercy will provide;
Trust, and thy trusting soul shall prove
Christ is its life and Christ its love.

Faint not nor fear, his arms are near;
He changeth not, and thou art dear;
Only believe, and thou shalt see
That Christ is all in all to thee.

WORDS: John Samuel Bewley Monsell (1811–1875)
MUSIC: From H. Boyd's Psalm and Hymn Tunes (1973), later attributed
to J. Hatton (d. 1793)

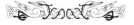

◈ *Reflections* ◈

My childhood ended abruptly on 31 May 1973. In the blur of pain after my brother Siggy's death, I remember little except helping to choose this hymn for his funeral. Five years younger than me, the fourth child of five, he had been knocked down by a lorry as he crossed the road outside his school playing fields a few days before his twelfth birthday.

He fought hard for life. For three days he lay in Glasgow's Western Infirmary, terribly injured but hanging on long enough for us to hope he might make it. It was that battle for life which was in our minds as we flicked through the hymn-book the next day, my mother so white and gaunt I could hardly bear to look at her, my father silently pacing backwards and forwards across the room.

"Fight the good fight" caught my eye, and with little more thought than that this was surely the hymn for our boy, we chose it. It was only when I rose to sing it a couple of days later in tiny Baldernock church, stricken at the sight of the small coffin resting at the spot where parents normally stood to bring their lively children for baptism, that I realised what the rest of the hymn was telling us to do. Amid the waste of death, we found ourselves singing "Lay hold on life". Deep in the misery of the sight of that still coffin, we heard ourselves murmuring, "Lift up thine eyes". In a haze of grief we sang of trusting to the love of Christ and a meaning to human existence where there seemed at that moment to be none at all.

Sometimes a hymn gets there before you.

◈

7. JUST AS A SINGLE FLOWER

1. Just as a single flower
springs upwards from the earth,
pure in the morning hour,
innocent of its birth;
then, by the scythe invaded,
lies in a moment's span,
leaves dead and colour faded –
so ends the life of man.

3. Death, with his reaper's sickle,
to beauty pays no heed;
his random strokes and fickle
spare neither flower nor weed.
Blossoms in summer splendour,
grasses or herbs or sedge,
all must to him surrender
and fall to his sickle's edge.

10. Our great Redeemer, Jesus,
now sits on heaven's throne.
With watchful eye he sees us
and cares for all his own.
Victor o'er Death, by dying
himself upon the tree,
for ever justifying
a sinner such as me.

13. His name through life shall stay me,
and soothe my dying breath;
though health and heart betray me,
I shall not shrink from Death.
O Death, no more I dread thee,

Just as a single flower

for all thy might and power;
but in Christ's strength I bid thee
welcome, whate'er the hour.

WORDS: Hallgrímur Pétursson (1614–1674)
TRANSLATION: Adapted by Magnus Magnusson from versions by
Arthur Charles Gook (*Hymns of the Passion*, Reykjavík, 1978) and
G. M. Gathorne-Hardy (in *An Anthology of Icelandic Poetry*,
ed. Eiríkur Benedikz, Reykjavík, 1969)
MUSIC: Adapted from a Good Friday hymn-tune from the Low Countries,
which reached Iceland in the sixteenth century

❦❧ *Reflections* ❦❧

No one understood the convulsive effect of the death of a child better than the Icelandic hymn-writer Hallgrímur Pétursson. If my brother had died in Iceland, home of our forefathers, this would have been the hymn which accompanied him to his grave. It is sung at every Icelandic funeral, a tradition which began in 1633 when the exquisite "*Allt eins og blómstrið eina*" ("Just as a single flower") was heard at a graveside for the first time when young Ragneiður Brynjólfsdóttir, daughter of the Bishop of Skálholt, was laid to rest.

The seventeenth century was the darkest in that northerly nation's history, a period of unremitting destitution, famine and foreign depredation. Before he met her, Hallgrímur's own wife Guðrún had been snatched from Iceland by Moorish pirates and sold as a concubine in the slave-markets of Algiers, fortunately to be returned nine years later with other survivors on payment of a ransom by the king of Denmark. Hallgrímur kept his family by hiring himself out for seasonal fishing and farm labour, until the Bishop of Skálholt, who had spotted exceptional academic potential, took him under his wing and ordained him to the Lutheran ministry. The poetry of spiritual hope and humanity which later burst from Hallgrímur Pétursson still blazes out of that soulless century like a lighthouse.

Hallgrímur's later cycle of fifty *Hymns of the Passion* (see page 52) earned him a place in Iceland's literary pantheon which he still occupies, but it is the poem he wrote after the death of his daughter, just short of her fourth birthday around 1649, which continues to accompany Icelanders to their graves today. Hallgrímur had already lost two children in infancy and little Steinunn was his treasure. His hymn is a long meditation, thirteen verses in all, on the mutability of life and the defeat of death by the resurrected Christ.

Death, he reminds us, pays no heed to beauty or to youth: flower, weed, grasses, herbs and sedge all fall to that indiscriminate sickle. But the bereaved father is ready in the end to outface it. "In Christ's strength," he says quietly to Death, "I bid thee welcome".

Hallgrímur Pétursson

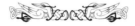

8. KING OF GLORY, KING OF PEACE

King of glory, king of peace,
  I will love thee;
And that love may never cease,
  I will move thee.
Thou hast granted my request,
  Thou hast heard me;
Thou didst note my working breast,
  Thou hast spared me.

Wherefore with my utmost art
  I will sing thee,
And the cream of all my heart
  I will bring thee.
Though my sins against me cried,
  Thou didst clear me;
And alone, when they replied,
  Thou didst hear me.

Seven whole days, not one in seven,
  I will praise thee;
In my heart, though not in heaven,
  I can raise thee.
Small it is, in this poor sort
  To enrol thee:
E'en eternity's too short
  To extol thee.

WORDS: George Herbert (1593–1633)
MUSIC: "Gwalchmai" by J. D. Jones (1827–1870)

⚄⚄ *Reflections* ⚄⚄

Studying English Literature at Edinburgh University in my early twenties, I discovered George Herbert and his spiky co-religionist John Donne. The poetry of these seventeenth-century "metaphysical" poets was like being doused in an invigorating shower: dramatic, personal, witty and ingeniously wrought. Each of them made poetry out of argument, both with himself and with God, but Herbert was the more subtly musical, less of a show-off in his versifying, more meditative. Perhaps that is why a number of his poems, like this one, have become hymns.

Herbert was a well-born scholar who gave up hopes of preferment at court to take Holy Orders in the Anglican priesthood. Many of his poems bear a remarkably modern sense of struggle, although the ones which were later adopted for congregational singing tend to be the less rebellious ones (which for those of us who enjoy an argument may be a pity). No one, as far as I am aware, has set to music the achingly heartfelt "Deniall":

> *O that thou should giv'st dust a tongue*
> > *To crie to thee,*
> *And then not heare it crying! all day long*
> > *My heart was in my knee,*
> > *But no hearing.*

But even in his most serene verse, the presence of a man who has wrestled with the fallibilities of his humanity can be felt. In the famous hymn "Let all the world in every corner sing", George Herbert the man is there in the lines:

> *But above all, the heart*
> *Must bear the longest part.*

"King of glory, king of peace" finds Herbert harnessing the deceptive simplicity of his art for one purpose alone: praise. I love the innate musicality of this hymn. I relish the single syllables punched home in every second line: "I will sing thee"…"Thou didst hear me"…"I can raise thee." I thrill to the physicality of the fresh country metaphor,

> *And the cream of all my heart*
> *I will bring thee.*

Four hundred years on, this is my kind of hymn.

9. CHIEF OF CHIEFS

Chief of chiefs beyond my ken,
  O Chief of chiefs, Amen.

God be with me lying down,
  And God be with me rising,
In the sunlight flying down
  God with me, supervising,
No joy nor any light without him,
  Nor any light without him.

Christ be with me sleeping hours,
  And Christ be with me waking,
Through all watches aiding powers,
  Christ with me undertaking,
No day nor any night without him,
  Nor any night without him.

God be with me to protect,
  The Spirit there to strengthen,
Lord be with me to direct
  As span of life doth lengthen,
No time, no year, no hope, no fear,
No age, no space, no work, no place,
No depth nor any height without him,
  Nor any height without him.

Ever, evermore, Amen,
  O Chief of chiefs, Amen.

WORDS: Traditional Gaelic song from Kintail and Harris

⚅⚅ *Reflections* ⚅⚅

Ihave never heard it sung. I have no idea what melody or what instruments accompanied this most loving song of the Gaels to their God. But even silent and in translation, something of the lyrical ardour of the original lingers. I fancy I can almost hear the refrain in my head, lilting to some ethereal tune not of man's making at all: "No joy nor any light without him… No day nor any night without him… No depth nor any height without him."

The poem comes from a body of oral Gaelic literature collected and translated at the turn of the last century by Dr Alexander Carmichael, who spent long periods in the Scottish Highlands and Islands transcribing poems, songs and prayers from the lips of Highlanders themselves, most of which reach back to a time before the ill-fated Jacobite Rebellion of 1745 and the subsequent break-up of the clans.

The spiritual outpouring of those Gaels is one of extraordinary richness and grace. This poem, which Dr Carmichael picked up around Kintail and Harris, needs only a thoughtful musical arrangement to become a truly glorious hymn. How satisfying that people living lives of physical hardship in dank, stone-and-turf cottages on the extremities of Britain long ago, who rose with the sun and slept as the peatfire died, can offer the twenty-first century timeless insights into the nature and immanence of God. The image of God as chief of chiefs is strikingly apt: to a Highland clansman the chief was prince, hero, protector and father of his people, all in one. In its directness, its economy and its masterful distillation of the assertion that nothing in all creation can separate us from the love of God, this is a hymn to rival any in the English tradition.

My own great-grandmother, Annie McKechnie, was a Gaelic-speaking Highlander from the isle of Mull, whose family had been driven off their croft in the 1860s by a landowner bent on making money from sheep. Annie was later sent south to serve as a parlourmaid in a mansion in Ayrshire, where she married a joiner on the estate by the name of James Baird; their third son, John Baird, who later married a young French polisher by the name of Sarah Greig, was my grandfather. When my mother used to visit Annie as a child, the old lady was still singing Gaelic songs, rocking on her chair in a Rutherglen tenement far from the islands and weeping, as she sang, for a life past and a heritage lost.

Suppression, neglect and finally geography have nudged the culture of Gaeldom into what is probably irrecoverable decline. But thanks to the far-sighted enthusiasm of collectors like Dr Carmichael and his family, some of the ancient riches are still accessible – not least this distant whisper from men and women who once sang for God to be with them in the flying sunlight and the sleeping night.

10. JERUSALEM

And did those feet in ancient time
Walk upon England's mountains green?
And was the holy Lamb of God
On England's pleasant pastures seen?

And did the countenance divine
Shine forth upon our clouded hills?
And was Jerusalem builded here
Among those dark satanic mills?

Bring me my bow of burning gold!
Bring me my arrows of desire!
Bring me my spear! O clouds, unfold!
Bring me my chariot of fire!

I will not cease from mental fight,
Nor shall my sword sleep in my hand,
Till we have built Jerusalem
In England's green and pleasant land.

WORDS: William Blake (1757–1827)
MUSIC: Hubert Parry (1848–1918)

Reflections

It is always alarming when politics hijacks a hymn. When the Prime Minister declares that "Jerusalem" is his favourite hymn because it is symbolic of his feelings for New Labour, you either want to toss Tony Blair his spear, climb into that chariot and urge him on with his mental fight, or you want to be quietly sick. In inclining to the latter I am aware of a certain hypocrisy, because what am I doing in this book if not appropriating hymns for their personal symbolism? But perhaps what I am reacting to is the suspicion that something of value is stolen from a hymn or a poem when it becomes the battle-cry of a movement rather than a cry from the soul.

But "Jerusalem" does lend itself to this kind of pillaging. Ever since Hubert Parry borrowed William Blake's words and added his famous tune to celebrate the cause of women's suffrage in 1916, I suspect the hymn has raised more roofs at Women's Institute meetings, Christian Socialist guilds and Promenade concerts than churches. It has virtually become a second English national anthem, although Scots are less enamoured with the last line.

So why do I like it, then? Partly because for a poem (from the 1804 preface to Blake's "Milton") which was to find itself gracing hymn-books over a hundred years later, it is in a class of its own. How cheering to find arrows of desire being summoned rather than banished. What a change to have to wrestle meaning, for once, from a hymn's imagery. Ultimately, though, the mysticism is too opaque for it to satisfy fully as a hymn. The tune is magnificent, but apart from a vague notion that the poet is fighting to create a new artistic order with his burning weapons of genius, it's not particularly clear what Blake is on about here – which is doubtless why "Jerusalem" so easily becomes whatever anyone wants to make of it.

— 41 —

It first began seeping into my consciousness in the early eighties when, as a young newspaper reporter, I wrote the biography of the Olympic athlete Eric Liddell to coincide with the release of the movie *Chariots of Fire*, which dramatises his story. After the British team's triumphant return from the 1924 Olympics in Paris, it is Blake's words and Parry's music which carry the film to its triumphant conclusion, ushering in the final credits over a moving reprise of the athletes pounding the white sands of St Andrews in their flapping running gear. Once again the hymn was being called into inspirational service, this time celebrating physical striving and achievement.

I doubt if the obscure metaphors of "Jerusalem" would have appealed much to the real Eric Liddell, whose faith was robustly literal. Soon after winning his gold medal in the 200 metres, he went off to the killing fields of China to confront flesh and blood swordwavers with the gospel of Jesus. But this protean hymn to human aspiration rather than divine inspiration reminds me of him all the same.

11. BE STILL, MY SOUL

Be still, my soul: the Lord is on thy side;
Bear patiently the cross of grief or pain;
Leave to thy God to order and provide;
In every change he faithful will remain.
Be still, my soul: thy best, thy heavenly friend
Through thorny ways leads to a joyful end.

Be still, my soul: thy God doth undertake
To guide the future as he has the past.
Thy hope, thy confidence let nothing shake;
All now mysterious shall be bright at last.
Be still, my soul: the waves and winds still know
His voice who ruled them while he dwelt below.

Be still, my soul: when dearest friends depart,
And all is darkened in the vale of tears,
Then shalt thou better know his love, his heart,
Who comes to soothe thy sorrow and thy fears.
Be still, my soul: thy Jesus can repay,
From his own fulness, all he takes away.

Be still, my soul: the hour is hastening on
When we shall be forever with the Lord,
When disappointment, grief, and fear are gone,
Sorrow forgot, love's purest joys restored.
Be still, my soul: when change and tears are past,
All safe and blessed we shall meet at last.

WORDS: Katherina von Schlegel (1697– c. 1768)
TRANSLATION: Jane L. Borthwick (1813–1897)
MUSIC: Jean Sibelius (1865–1957)

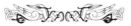

Reflections

If ever a hymn rejoiced in its music, it is this one. When a composer like Sibelius is orchestrating the emotion, even the least adventurous of Victorian clichés can tiptoe past, engulfed in the wave of sound. Thorny ways and vales of tears will almost pass for sublime when the music is.

This was the hymn which rang out one March day in 1945 at Weihsien internment camp in north-east China, just south of Beijing. Eric Liddell, missionary and former athlete, was being remembered at a memorial service almost two weeks after his death from a brain tumour. It had always been his favourite hymn, an appropriate one for a man whose last words before he slipped into a coma, were, "It's complete surrender". Fittingly for a hymn which the Lutheran Katherina von Schlegel wrote as a contribution to the Pietist revival in Germany, its theme is patient endurance of life's trials and confident resignation to the command of Psalm 46 to "Be still and know that I am God".

Liddell had given up sporting stardom to become a missionary teacher and then an itinerant evangelist in a country riven by civil war and under attack by the Japanese, who interned him in 1943. Twenty years earlier he had written of this hymn to his fiancée Florence: "I often play it over. It goes to the beautiful tune, *Finlandia* – a calm, restful tune." Under constant physical threat before internment and then amid the daily discomforts and mental stresses of life in camp, it continued to remind him of what mattered: that God, remaining faithful in every change, would order and provide. For a man suffering from blinding headaches, separated from his family, feeling even his personality under insidious attack from the illness, it was balm indeed to remember that

Then shalt thou better know his love, his heart,
Who comes to soothe thy sorrow and thy fears.
Be still, my soul: thy Jesus can repay,
From his own fulness, all he takes away.

On the afternoon of his death he scribbled a few snatches of thought on some scraps of paper. Among them were the four words, "Be still my soul", and a broken phrase or two from other parts of the hymn.

The words Eric Liddell scrawled on his last day on earth illustrate the extraordinary capacity of hymns to sink deep into the mind and then surface when all else is failing, even the mind itself. I may cavil at clichés, but as he faced eternity, a man was speaking to his soul in the words of this hymn. What greater evidence of potency is there than that?

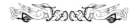

12. WE CANNOT MEASURE HOW YOU HEAL

We cannot measure how you heal
or answer every sufferer's prayer,
yet we believe your grace responds
where faith and doubt unite to care.
Your hands, though bloodied on the cross,
survive to hold and heal and warn,
to carry all through death to life
and cradle children yet unborn.

The pain that will not go away,
the guilt that clings from things long past,
the fear of what the future holds
are present as if meant to last.
But present too is love which tends
the hurt we never hoped to find,
the private agonies inside,
the memories that haunt the mind.

So some have come who need your help
and some have come to make amends,
as hands which shaped and saved the world
are present in the touch of friends.
Lord, let your Spirit meet us here
to mend the body, mind and soul,
to disentangle peace from pain
and make your broken people whole.

WORDS: John L. Bell and Graham Maule
MUSIC: "Ye Banks and Braes", Scottish traditional air

⚂⚂ *Reflections* ⚂⚂

I didn't exactly meet my husband on Iona, but I certainly met him through it. The tiny jewel of an island off the south-western toe of Mull is where Columba established a monastery in 563 AD and launched his Celtic missionary movement. It is also where a feisty Glasgow minister by the name of George MacLeod founded another Columban mission of sorts in 1938: the Iona Community. This is one of their hymns.

Minister at the time of Govan Old Parish Church, an area blighted by the Depression, MacLeod shared with Columba a belief that obedience to Christ meant taking the gospel out from monasteries and cathedrals, abbeys and churches, to the people. Iona's ancient legacy as an island where the spiritual and the material seemed within a wave's breath of one another inspired MacLeod to try to restore that wholeness to the witness of the Church. He brought unemployed craftsmen from Glasgow to rebuild the ruined Iona Abbey, alongside young ministers who were then sent out on a new urban ministry to working class communities.

The Iona Community continues to have its base on the island and its work out in the world among the deprived. In the same way, the hymns spawned by worship in the abbey have roots deep in the Celtic Christian tradition, but many also offer an assured articulation of the hopes and griefs of a modern century.

I first came across "We cannot measure how you heal" at a service in the town of Dunblane the Sunday after the massacre of its school-children in 1996. It is the ultimate test of a hymn to be invited to help traumatised people to express the inexpressible. This one, by the Iona Community hymn-writers John Bell and Graham Maule, did not fail. Sung to the traditional Scots air "Ye banks and braes", its sensitivity to the darkness of human experience did communicate something of Dunblane's dazed anguish that day. It also offered the hope of a mending of "body, mind and soul", a vision of ultimate wholeness which brought just a hint of the Celtic, the merest whisper of a wave from Iona, into the devastated cathedral.

I have visited Iona often, and enjoyed the hospitality of the Iona Community. But I'm sorry I never had the chance to tell its founder that he was inadvertently responsible for my marriage.

In the summer of 1982 Norman Stone, a young English film-maker, travelled to Iona to research a proposed drama about Columba. He then went on to Edinburgh to interview the elderly, but still endearingly roguish Lord MacLeod of Fuinary and, finding himself down the coast from Dundee, decided on the spur of the moment to try and catch a friend's play at an art festival there. He duly turned up that afternoon, a more eye-catching figure than Dundee was possibly ready for in his foppish London director's garb of leather jacket, white shoes and long, white, silken scarf. We were introduced at the play.

I confided to my mother the next day that I had met a most attractive guy, but that he wore white shoes and was probably gay. Happily for me and the offspring whose fate hung in the balance, he wasn't. Iona has been dear to our hearts ever since.

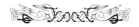

13. LOVE DIVINE

Love divine, all loves excelling,
Joy of heaven, to earth come down,
Fix in us thy humble dwelling,
All thy faithful mercies crown.
Jesu, thou are all compassion,
Pure unbounded love thou art;
Visit us with thy salvation,
Enter every trembling heart.

Come, almighty to deliver,
Let us all thy life receive;
Suddenly return, and never,
Never more thy temples leave.
Thee we would be always blessing,
Serve thee as thy hosts above,
Pray, and praise thee without ceasing,
Glory in thy perfect love.

Finish then thy new creation,
Pure and sinless let us be;
Let us see thy great salvation,
Perfectly restored in thee,
Changed from glory into glory,
Till in heaven we take our place,
Till we cast our crowns before thee,
Lost in wonder, love, and praise.

WORDS: Charles Wesley (1707-1788)
MUSIC: "Blaenwern" by W. P. Rowlands (1860–1937)

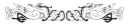

⚜ *Reflections* ⚜

Ah, Charles Wesley. A man with the ardour of a convert and the imagination of a poet. Of the nearly 6000 hymns he penned, this is surely the most exquisite.

Before his conversion he was an intense but ineffective clergyman, beleaguered by failures in his private life. Afterwards, he and his brother John Wesley, who had an equally dramatic revelation of personal salvation a few months later in May 1738, couldn't wait to take this freshly understood Gospel to everyone, not least the outcasts of society. Thousands poured into fields and purpose-built chapels to hear the message. One day hundreds of Bristol miners, the lowest of underclass life, stopped to listen to Wesley preach as they straggled up from their hell-hole underground. It was said that white streaks could be discerned on the coal-blackened faces as they stood around him. In such ways was Methodism born.

I first began to appreciate the mighty Methodist hymns when the new boyfriend, still in those shoes, took me to Cornwall to meet a deaf and blind poet by the name of Jack Clemo. I was touched to be introduced so early in our acquaintance to this veteran Cornish bard, only discovering later that "Come down and see my poet" was a novel twist on the etchings theme and that a steady stream of girlfriends had preceded me. Still, it was worth it for the look on Norman's face when Jack put his hand on my shoulder and fixed his dark glasses on my face with seer-like intensity, while his wife Ruth, uncannily able to interpret his every action, trilled meaningfully: "So this is the One at last, is it?"

Jack and Ruth lived in his tiny childhood cottage on the edge of the eerie white china clay-works at Goonamarris – "the dripping clay with which I am baptised" – which had inspired some of his most savagely memorable poetry. Along the road at Trethosa was the Methodist chapel. He had been worshipping there for more than sixty years, unseeing and unhearing for most of them, yet relishing the distant tremble of the Wesleyan hymns which he could feel through the vibration of the organ along the floor.

When he responded to a hymn like "Love divine", the rhythm at his feet, the words sounding deep inside his head, it was as if the same emotion, the same vibrancy of spirit which had enflamed Charles Wesley and brought hope to miners treated like animals were surging through Jack Clemo, too. The same faith, through all the obstacles he had encountered as a penniless, disabled writer in an obscure corner of England, enabled this man to sing with Wesley, soundlessly but passionately, of being "lost in wonder, love, and praise". The image of the crowns being cast before the Almighty is one of the most stunningly original evocations of heaven in any hymn.

I offered there and then to write Jack Clemo's biography. Long before I finished it, Norman had also come round to the view that I was the One.

14. Thou art, Lord Jesus, King Alone

(FROM PASSION HYMN 27)

9. Thou art, Lord Jesus, King alone,
ruler on heaven's eternal throne;
king of the angels, king of might,
king of everlasting light.

11. Lord Jesus, I confess to thee:
Thy merits are my only plea,
When time it is for all to meet
Before thine awful Judgement Seat.

13. Jesus, my Lord, I call thee king:
call me thy slave, thy meanest thing.
no worldly title here on earth
compares with such a name of worth.

15. Jesus, thine is the glory which I use,
Thine the kingdom which I choose.
May thy power ever increase
And lead us all to heavenly peace.

WORDS: Hallgrímur Pétursson (1614–1674)
TRANSLATION: Magnus Magnusson
MUSIC: Páll Ísólfsson (1893–1974)

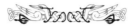

❧ *Reflections* ❧

The guests at our wedding in 1984 took one look at the Order of Service, then another. "O perfect love" they could handle and even the most irreligious of fellow hacks could make a stab at "The Lord's my Shepherd". But what was this?

> *Víst ertu, Jesú, kóngur klár,*
> *kóngur dýrðar um eilíf ár,*
> *kóngur englanna, kóngur vor,*
> *kóngur almættis tignarstór.*

Three more uncompromisingly Icelandic verses followed, and not even a translation

People doubtless guessed that the Scandinavian ancestry of one half of the bridal couple was responsible for the inclusion of these strangely accented words with the ancient Nordic letters; that along with all my Scottish relations and what appeared to be half the English town of Hartlepool on Norman's side, I was keen to have my Icelandic heritage represented. What they didn't know was how far the hymn, by Hallgrímur Pétursson, reached back into my childhood.

Visiting Iceland in the 1960s with my parents and younger sister Margaret, we were shown around a country church at Reykholt by the local MP, who as so often in a nation as small and multi-cultured as Iceland was not only a politician but also a songwriter, poet, playwright and bass-baritone. His name was Jónas Árnason. He offered to sing us something there and then, and after summoning the church organist, launched forth. The sun was pouring in from outside, washing the plain, wooden pews with light. A gang of blue-black flies buzzed fretfully against the windows, while over us rolled that voice, rich and deep, singing with electrifying conviction of *Jesú kóngur*, Jesus the king.

— 53 —

Only later did I learn that the song was from Hallgrímur Pétursson's *Passion Hymns*, a sequence which took Iceland's finest hymn-writer three years, from 1656 to 1659, to write. Each one is inspired by an episode in the passion and death of Christ, and in each Hallgrímur enters both Christ's agony and the sufferings of ordinary people.

Víst ertu, Jesú belongs to the second half of Hymn 27, where the poet breaks into a triumphant address to Christ. Much of its power resides in the music, which filled the church at Reykholt that day and our Baldernock kirk again in 1984. It is based on an old Gregorian chant which the Icelandic composer Páll Ísólfsson heard an old man in the north humming on his deathbed and adapted to fit Hallgrímur's words.

The wedding guests made a game attempt at their first Icelandic hymn. We didn't quite emulate Jónas Árnason, but I will never forget the sound of those plangent Icelandic cadences seeping into the stones of a Scottish church which had never heard the like before.

Norman and I on our Wedding Day

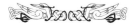

15. O PERFECT LOVE

O perfect Love, all human thought transcending,
Lowly we kneel in prayer before thy throne,
That theirs may be the love which knows no ending
Whom thou for evermore dost join in one.

O perfect Life, be thou their full assurance
Of tender charity and steadfast faith,
Of patient hope, and quiet brave endurance,
With childlike trust that fears nor pain nor death.

Grant them the joy which brightens earthly sorrow;
Grant them the peace which calms all earthly strife,
And to life's day the glorious unknown morrow
That dawns upon eternal love and life.

WORDS: Dorothy Frances Gurney (1858–1932)
MUSIC: "Perfect Love (Sandringham)" by Joseph Barnby (1838–1896)

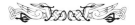

⚜ *Reflections* ⚜

We sang this hymn at a later point in the wedding service, after the marriage vows and at the conclusion of a witty and admirably practical address from Reverend Will Storrar, who drew our attention to the folly of storing up marital grievances. In front of my father, who was beaming in the front row, he reminded us of the scene in the Icelandic medieval masterpiece *Njál's Saga*, where the hero Gunnar is besieged by enemies in his house and asks his wife for two locks of her hair to plait into an emergency string for his broken bow.

"Does anything depend on it?" demands the haughty Hallgerður.

"My life depends on it," Gunnar replies, "for they will never overcome me as long as I can use my bow."

"In that case," says Hallgerður, chill as steel, "I shall now remind you of the slap you once gave me. I don't care in the least whether you hold out a long time or not."

Without his bow Gunnar was overwhelmed, and his mother pronounced Hallgerður an evil woman whose shame would be long remembered.

It was certainly remembered during our wedding service – and has featured with regrettable frequency ever since, most recently in an exchange which began: "So you want the car keys, do you? Then let me remind you of the time, only yesterday, when you reversed into my film editor's classic MG midget..." From which you will gather that "doing a Hallgerður" is neither gender-specific nor as fully expunged from our marriage as the minister might have wished.

Anyway, there we were at the end of the wedding address, heads reeling with the dark consquences of marital vengeance, when the organ introduced by way of finale the calm melody of "O perfect love".

It was written in 1883 by Dorothy Gurney, daughter of a London vicar, in response to a challenge from her sister to provide words suitable for a wedding to accompany a hymn-tune of which she was particularly fond. According to her own account, Mrs Gurney then nipped into the library and dashed off "O perfect love" in fifteen minutes. After being sung at her sister's nuptials, it became a popular fixture on the London wedding scene, eventually receiving its present tune from Sir Joseph Barnby for the wedding of George V's daughter Princess Louise of Wales to the Duke of Fife.

In choosing it for my own wedding, I was a little alarmed at its litany of homely Victorian values – strong meat for someone who had been careful to remove the word "obey" from her marriage vows. But as Norman and I stood side by side in the church, gingerly twisting our new gold bands, it was unexpectedly moving to hear being sung around us the prayer that we be granted joy to brighten the sorrow when it came and peace to calm any marital strife that might happen our way.

O perfect love

Baldernock Church

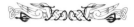

16. LEAD, KINDLY LIGHT

Lead, kindly light, amid the encircling gloom,
*   Lead thou me on;*
The night is dark, and I am far from home,
*   Lead thou me on.*
Keep thou my feet; I do not ask to see
The distant scene; one step enough for me.

I was not ever thus, nor prayed that thou
Should'st lead me on;
I loved to choose and see my path; but now
*   Lead thou me on.*
I loved the garish day, and, spite of fears,
Pride ruled my will: remember not past years.

So long thy power hath blessed me, sure it still
*   Will lead me on,*
O'er moor and fen, o'er crag and torrent, till
*   The night is gone;*
And with the morn those angel faces smile,
Which I have loved long since, and lost awhile.

WORDS: John Henry Newman (1801–1890)
MUSIC: "Sandon" by C. H. Purday

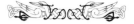

🧶 *Reflections* 🧶

The greatest hymns cannot be caged within one religious tradition. They burst across denominations and seize us before we can hoist our doctrinal colours or retreat to the strongholds of declared taste. Just as Charles Wesley's "Love divine, all loves excelling" was the hymn which rolled over Westminster Cathedral at the climax of Cardinal Basil Hume's funeral mass in 1999, so it is from the Roman Catholic Cardinal John Henry Newman that we have one of the most universally satisfying expressions of religious doubt and faltering submission to divine providence.

Some people never recover from the first line. D. H. Lawrence consigned this hymn to a category he regarded as "sentimental messes", and I suspect the word "kindly" had something to do with it. But I'm convinced that the adjective is artfully chosen. "Kindly" is a domestic, intimate, grandfatherly word, deliberately far removed from the lexicon of ecclesiastical posturing and abstruse debate which Newman, one of the great Christian thinkers himself, implies are as likely to obfuscate as to illumine what is ultimately important.

He wrote the hymn in 1833, 12 years before he joined the Church of Rome and long before he became a cardinal, at a time when he was beset by uncertainties about his faith and his position in the Church of England. It is a cry of humility from a man of proud and subtle intellect, a prayer for divine guidance over the stones and waterfalls of the mind. The writer Paul Johnson has suggested, in what I assume to be a spirit of self-deprecation, that it ought to be sung regularly "by all Christian intellectuals with a tendency to grow too big for their boots".

Perhaps that is what kept Basil Hume so humble. Asked near the end of his life to choose his favourite hymn, this twentieth-century cardinal named this one. He was too ill at the time to elaborate the reasons, but those around him knew instantly why he had chosen "Lead, kindly light". An adviser explained that these three words were the core of his life and spirit; he had never taken himself too seriously and bent his whole mind on the great light, Jesus Christ.

It is quietly satisfying that a hymn born out of religious divisions should offer the only possible way of transcending them.

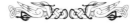

17. GREAT IS THY FAITHFULNESS

Great is thy faithfulness, O God my Father,
There is no shadow of turning with thee;
Thou changest not, thy compassions, they fail not;
As thou hast been thou for ever wilt be:

Great is thy faithfulness! Great is thy faithfulness!
Morning by morning new mercies I see;
All I have needed thy hand has provided.
Great is thy faithfulness, Lord, unto me.

Summer and winter, and springtime and harvest,
Sun, moon and stars in their courses above,
Join with all nature in manifold witness
To thy great faithfulness, mercy and love:

Pardon for sin and a peace that endureth,
Thy own dear presence to cheer and to guide;
Strength for today and bright hope for tomorrow,
Blessings all mine, with ten thousand beside!

WORDS: Thomas O. Chisholm (1866–1960)
MUSIC: William Runyan (1870–1957)

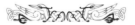

🖂 *Reflections* 🖂

For 10 years I was a Methodist. Having set up home near Maidenhead in Berkshire, Norman and I found ourselves one Sunday morning outside the Methodist church at the top of the High Street, wondering what a wandering Baptist and a refugee from the Church of Scotland would find there. By the end of the service we knew we had a place to worship for the remainder of our time in the south-east of England.

Thus began my real education in the hymns of Methodism. I'm afraid I never succeeded in identifying them by their number in the Methodist hymn book, a failure which brands me a mere parvenue among cradle Methodists, but I learned to appreciate them. And none more than "Great is thy faithfulness", a hymn I will always associate with that gentle church and the people who, in true Wesleyan spirit, made it such a welcoming place to all.

I can't remember if we encountered the hymn on that first crisp autumn Sunday. I like to think we did. We certainly sang it so often afterwards that it became almost a theme tune – literally so, in fact, when a video I presented about the church featured it in the opening sequence. Written by Thomas Chisholm, an American Methodist minister, it lacks the theological sophistication and poetic flair of the Wesley hymns, but shares the verve I appreciated among the Methodists. It celebrates the enduring constancy of God with energy and style.

I looked at the video the other day. True to my vain profession I spent the first few seconds wondering whether advanced pregnancy provided a good enough excuse for having worn a coat three sizes too big which made me look like a potato. Then I heard the chords of the hymn and was transported back to that place, and to those early years of marriage and that blithe celebration of God's faithfulness. If one function of hymns is to give us the words we could never find ourselves, another is to remind us of the things we once knew, and have sometimes forgotten.

Norman thinks they sang it on the Sunday morning that our first baby was born in December 1985. After a long and at one point dangerous night, he drove straight to church from the hospital, disshevelled and emotional, to give thanks for the safe arrival of our eldest son. Glancing at his feet during the service, he suddenly noticed a fetching arrangement of blood on his favourite white shoes. He never wore them again, alas.

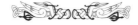

18. O FOR A THOUSAND TONGUES

O for a thousand tongues to sing
My great Redeemer's praise,
The glories of my God and King,
The triumphs of his grace!

My gracious Master and my God,
Assist me to proclaim
And spread through all the earth abroad
The honours of thy name.

Jesus! the name that charms our fears,
That bids our sorrows cease;
'Tis music in the sinner's ears,
'Tis life and health and peace.

He breaks the power of cancelled sin,
He sets the prisoner free;
His blood can make the foulest clean,
His blood availed for me.

He speaks, and, listening to his voice
New life the dead receive,
The mournful, broken hearts rejoice,
The humble poor believe.

Hear him, ye deaf; his praise, ye dumb,
Your loosened tongues employ;
Ye blind, behold your Saviour come;
And leap, ye lame, for joy!

Glory to God, and praise, and love
Be ever, ever given
By saints below and saints above,
The Church in earth and heaven.

WORDS: Charles Wesley (1707–1788). MUSIC: "Lyngham" by T. Jarman (1782–1862)

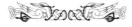

ᚎᚎ *Reflections* ᚎᚎ

As babies continued to arrive fast and furious, turning my days into a blur of nappies and nights into a dream of sleep, it was a relief to go out to work now and then. Mostly that meant anchoring the BBC's *Breakfast News* (if you're up half the night anyway, why not head for the newsroom at 4am and make a day of it?), but the most bizarre offers of escape came from the other programme I presented regularly, *Songs of Praise*, and one of the producers, Chris Mann.

"You want me to present from a train? Oh, I see there'll be a choir with me. And I have to meet up with Cliff Michelmore in another moving train and be recorded by his camera shouting my words through the window as we pass? And then travel half way round England? Oh, but I can feed the baby at St Pancras before we go, can I, while another choir is practising 'O for a thousand tongues' on the platform? Right. Fine. Jolly good. See you there, Chris."

That was in 1988, the 250th anniversary of John and Charles Wesley's conversion, which the BBC's popular hymn programme celebrated by persuading British Rail to send three trains simultaneously around the English towns most closely associated with the brothers' ministry. We drew away from St Pancras to the unforgettable swelling of what must have been nigh on a thousand tongues singing of the glories of their God and King, in the midst of which one three-month-old baby was doubtless wondering where his next feed was coming from.

It is a hymn made for big voices, an exuberant, exultant song of praise, which Charles Wesley is said to have written to celebrate the anniversary of his conversion on Whit Sunday 1738. Sung by a full congregation, with men and women laying their voices against each other, it is a hymn which can raise spirits and focus worship like nothing else.

Choirs love it. The renowned Glasgow Orpheus Choir under their director Sir Hugh Roberton probably had it in their repertoire, but they also popularised a pawky satirical poem which was sung to the same tune. There was an old tradition in Scotland of substituting nonsense words for a hymn in week-day rehearsal, so that the sacred words would not be demeaned by being uttered in a frivolous context outside the Sabbath: no conductor would wish to have to inform the tenors that their great Redeemer was off-key.

So in joyous four-part harmony to the tune "Lyngham", the Orpheus sang a centuries-old ditty mocking the Sabbatarian strictness of Scots Presbyterians, the last verse of which was added, with a nod to Robert Burns, by Roberton himself.

> *There was an auld Seceder cat*
> *And it was unco grey.*
> *It brought a mouse intae the kirk*
> *Upon the Sabbath day.*
>
> *They took it to the Session,*
> *Wha it rebuked sair,*
> *And made it promise faithfully*
> *Tae dae the same nae mair.*
>
> *And noo a' Sabbath day it sits*
> *Like some aul clockin' hen*
> *And canna understaun' ava'*
> *The weys o'mice and men.*

In the long history of Christian discord, it is hard to beat the bitter, though often bravely principled schisms within the Presbyterian church. If Wesley's hymn emphasises the true focus, then the rhyme which stole its tune gently restores a sense of humour.

19. ALL CREATURES OF OUR GOD AND KING

All creatures of our God and King,
Lift up your voice and with us sing
Alleluia, Alleluia!
Thou burning sun with golden beam,
Thou silver moon with softer gleam:
    O praise him, O praise him,
    Alleluia, Alleluia, Alleluia

Thou rushing wind that art so strong,
Ye clouds that sail in heaven along,
O praise him, Alleluia!
Thou rising morn, in praise rejoice,
Ye lights of evening, find a voice:

Thou flowing water, pure and clear,
Make music for thy Lord to hear,
Alleluia, Alleluia!
Thou fire so masterful and bright,
That givest man both warmth and light:

Dear mother earth, who day by day
Unfoldest blessings on our way,
O praise him, Alleluia!
The flowers and fruits that in thee grow,
Let them his glory also show:

And all ye men of tender heart,
Forgiving others, take your part,
O sing ye, Alleluia!
Ye who long pain and sorrow bear,
Praise God and on him cast your care:

And thou, most kind and gentle death,
Waiting to hush our latest breath,
O praise him, Alleluia!
Thou leadest home the child of God,
And Christ our Lord the way hath trod:

Let all things their Creator bless,
And worship him in humbleness,
O praise him, Alleluia!
Praise, praise the Father, praise the Son,
And praise the Spirit, three in One:
O praise him, O praise him,
Alleluia, Alleluia, Alleluia

WORDS: St Francis of Assissi (1182–1226)
TRANSLATION: William Henry Draper (1855–1933)
MELODY: From Geistliche Kirchengesang, Cologne, 1623.
Arranged by Ralph Vaughan Williams (1872–1958)

❦ *Reflections* ❦

During the countless school assemblies and Sunday School renditions it has been my cheerful duty to sit through as a parent, many a hymn has come my way. Some have merely reinforced a curmudgeonly strain in my personality which is resistant to even the most winsome of young voices trilling "All things bright and beautiful", a hymn written for children which a lot of adults seem unaccountably to love. But "All creatures of our God and King", composed (according to the first-hand evidence of his disciple Thomas of Celano) by St Francis of Assisi eight centuries ago, is not nearly so twee. Children enjoy it, but it's a grown-up hymn.

True, the translation suffers from the rhyming affliction which decrees that a rushing wind so strong will inevitably end up propelling clouds that sail in heaven along. And what would nineteenth-century writers and translators have done without "trod" to rhyme with "God"? All the same, the drama of St Francis's original canticle is still there, his lyrical command to all things to worship their Creator. The lights of evening are urged to find a voice, the flowing water to make music, the flowers to show their glory and suffering humanity to join in the praise, while even death itself, arrestingly cast in the same lovable role as the rest of the ensemble, is instructed to lead its souls to God. This is a hymn with charm, which is not the same as sentimentality.

I'm glad that children do still learn it, though. It is meatier fare than the mushy diet they are often fed these days. Children in times past may have understood little of the sonorous hymns they were expected to memorise, but at least these stayed in their minds to be savoured and understood later. At her primary school in Rutherglen, my mother learned by heart:

O God of Bethel! by whose hand
Thy people still are fed,
Who through this weary pilgrimage
Hast all our fathers led.

She often wondered who exactly it was who threw this weary pil-grimage, but the puzzle didn't stop her remembering the hymn for a lifetime.

Children these days are fortunate if they have any access to hymns at all, so perhaps I shouldn't quibble about range and depth. But it will be sad if there is nothing ancient and comfortable and inspirational amid the furniture of their minds to relax into when they are older. I hope at least that "All creatures of our God and King" will be there.

My mother, Mamie Baird

20. PRAISE, MY SOUL, THE KING OF HEAVEN

Praise, my soul, the King of heaven;
To his feet thy tribute bring;
Ransomed, healed, restored, forgiven,
Who like me his praise should sing?
 Praise him! Praise him!
 Praise him! Praise him!
Praise the everlasting King.

Praise him for his grace and favour
To our fathers in distress;
Praise him, still the same for ever,
Slow to chide and swift to bless:
 Praise him! Praise him!
 Praise him! Praise him!
Glorious in his faithfulness.

Father-like he tends and spares us;
Well our feeble frame he knows;
In his hands he gently bears us,
Rescues us from all our foes:
 Praise him! Praise him!
 Praise him! Praise him!
Widely as his mercy flows.

Frail as summer's flower we flourish,
Blows the wind and it is gone;
But, while mortals rise and perish,
God endures unchanging on:
 Praise him! Praise him!
 Praise him! Praise him!
Praise the high eternal One.

Angels, help us to adore him;
Ye behold him face to face;
Sun and moon, bow down before him,
Dwellers all in time and space.
   Praise him! Praise him!
   Praise him! Praise him!
Praise with us the God of grace.

WORDS: Henry Francis Lyte (1793–1847), based on Psalm 103
MUSIC: John Goss (1800–1880)

⫴ *Reflections* ⫴

In the spring of 1995, with a fifth baby on the way, we left our heaving cottage in London's crowded commuter belt by the Thames and set up home in rural Scotland, just outside the parish of Baldernock where I grew up.

What a pleasure to be back: to spot small, white-rumped deer skittering into the gorse on the hill behind our house, to learn to avoid frogs and rabbits on the road again, to admire the lethal majesty of the buzzards swooping overhead and the springtime frenzy of the lapwings. I reacquainted myself with the rhythm of the farming seasons, on land and in church festivals (although sadly pulpits hereabouts no longer ring to the sort of weather-specific prayer which an old Baldernock minister is said to have offered on behalf of farmers and their rain-sodden crops: "Oh Lord, we pray thee to send us wind – no' a rantin', tantin', ravin' wind, but a hoochin', soochin', winnin' wind.") I also derived an intoxicating pleasure from the profusion of wild flowers – wayside weeds, if you must – which blossomed and danced and died along the paths around us.

> *Frail as summer's flower we flourish,*
> *Blows the wind and it is gone.*

You cannot live in the countryside for long without being keenly aware of the cycle of birth, decay and regeneration which animates Henry Lyte in his spirited paraphrase of Psalm 103. "Praise, my soul, the King of heaven" sets the perishability of all created things, even the stars and the planets, "dwellers all in time and space", against the immutable presence of God himself.

Henry Lyte is the Brixham vicar who later wrote the elegiac "Abide with me" (see page 113). Like that hymn "Praise, my soul, the King of heaven" is in the debt of its musical arrangement, but the words hold their own. I doubt if you'll find a more masterly line of theological distillation than "Ransomed, healed, restored, forgiven". Nor a more economical rendering of the psalmist's metaphor of mortality than Lyte's image of the frail summer flower succumbing to a good drying breeze of the kind that farmers pray for: "Blows the wind", he says "and it is gone."

Just as David, the psalmist, ends Psalm 103 with an injunction to praise the Lord for all his works throughout his dominion, so Lyte's achievement is to cap his understated image of evanescence with a picture of the universe itself bowing down before the unchangeable God. In its unpretentious way, the hymn is a masterpiece.

21. SOUL OF MY SAVIOUR

Soul of my Saviour, sanctify my breast,
Body of Christ, be thou my saving guest,
Blood of my Saviour, bathe me in thy tide,
Wash me with water flowing from thy side.

Strength and protection may thy Passion be,
O blessed Jesus, hear and answer me;
Deep in thy wounds, Lord, hide and shelter me,
So shall I never, never part from thee.

Guard and defend me from the foe malign,
In death's dread moments make me only thine;
Call me and bid me come to thee on high,
Where I may praise thee with thy saints for aye.

WORDS: Attributed to Pope John XII (1249–1334)
TRANSLATION: from Latin unknown
MUSIC: "Anima Christi" by William Joseph Maher (1832–1877)

The small, white-washed Church of Scotland kirk in the village where we made our new home has an inclusive approach to song. On a Sunday morning you might find yourself singing anything from arm-waving children's verses to breezy choruses and thoughtfully updated psalms, right through to the grandest hymns of old. But nowhere will you encounter this one.

I happened upon it only when I began idly asking friends and colleagues about their favourite hymn. Emphatically, and without a moment's thought, several of a Roman Catholic persuasion chose "Soul of my Saviour". I had never heard of it, and was so intrigued that I sought out a CD of Catholic religious music and listened, discovering in the process a host (as it were) of hymns which were all new to me.

The iconography makes it obvious why these have not travelled across denominational borders. "Soul of my Saviour" is a poetic affirmation of the distinctively Catholic understanding of the mystery of the mass, or as one friend put it, "of what we have just received – the body, blood, soul and divinity of Christ Jesus". For this reason it is usually sung in thanksgiving afterwards and makes no claim to be the sort of hymn which any believer would wish to sing anywhere. The surprise to me is that despite having no stomach for strong crucifixion imagery and belonging to a tradition uncomfortable with the idea of sharing its praise with saints, I have come to like this hymn very much. The more I listen, the more the simple majesty of it grows on me. This is partly, no doubt, because of the musical setting – the tune is a lovely one – but also because the prayer at its heart expands from private musings over the mass to a more universal plea for the eternal embrace of God. I begin to see why so many people have booked it for their funerals.

The late Auberon Waugh, devoted iconoclast, wrote of being profoundly moved in his youth when "Soul of my Saviour" was sung by "raucous adolescent broken voices" at his public school. (He claimed also to have become immoderately excited when, for reasons unconnected with personal devotion, he had heard the first line sung by women.) Even in famously cantakerous adulthood and despite finding the hymn "slightly incoherent", he still considered it his favourite. It remains special to many Catholics, even relatively young ones who prefer it to the folksy songs which have overtaken much of their formal worship.

Scottish patriots are also fond of recollecting, mischievously no doubt, that it is thought to have been penned by John XII, the Pope who recognised Scottish independence in 1320 after the Declaration of Arbroath.

I would like to sing it myself one day. Since the Reformation excludes me from mass and it from a Kirk communion, I suspect I never will.

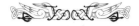

22. IN THE BLEAK MID-WINTER

In the bleak mid-winter,
Frosty wind made moan,
Earth stood hard as iron,
Water like a stone;
Snow had fallen, snow on snow,
Snow on snow,
In the bleak mid-winter,
Long ago.

Our God, heaven cannot hold him,
Nor earth sustain;
Heaven and earth shall flee away
When he comes to reign;
In the bleak mid-winter
A stable-place sufficed
The Lord God Almighty,
Jesus Christ.

Angels and archangels
May have gathered there,
Cherubim and seraphim
Thronged the air;
But his mother only,
In her maiden bliss,
Worshipped the Beloved
With a kiss.

What can I give him,
Poor as I am?
If I were a shepherd,
I would bring a lamb;
If I were a wise man,

In the bleak mid-winter

I would do my part;
Yet what I can I give him –
Give my heart.

WORDS: Christina Rossetti (1830–1894)
MUSIC: Gustav Holst (1874–1934)

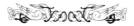

Reflections

I love Christmas carols – all of them – which is just as well, since my husband embraces festivals with such exuberance that the house is filled with strains of the First Nowell almost as soon as Guy Fawkes night is over. Autumn leaves may be drifting off the trees, the city streets still discreetly dark, but those herald angels are out in force in our kitchen, and there they stay until the end of the year.

Like most people, I rarely pay much attention to what the carols are saying, which is probably just as well in a number of cases, although Charles Wesley's "Hark! the herald angels sing" is as rich as you would expect from him. It is rather the aroma of Christmas which matters, the memories the hymns evoke, the gleam of childlike wonder that still flashes somewhere deep inside at the mere mention of a stable and a sky filled with seraphim.

One carol which does bear inspection, though, is "In the bleak midwinter" by the pre-Raphaelite poet Christina Rossetti. True, the original Middle Eastern nativity players would have been considerably astonished if snow had really fallen, snow on snow, on the night of Christ's birth. But no matter. This is a poem with an internal logic. The scene it sets with a few deft strokes is our winter, our Christmas, a time when

> *Earth stood hard as iron,*
> *Water like a stone.*

Christina Rossetti is thought to have composed the words while staying at Penkill Castle in Ayrshire, a favourite Scottish holiday retreat of the set of nineteenth-century painters and poets known as the pre-Raphaelites, who included among others her brother Dante Gabriel Rossetti, William Holman Hunt, William Morris and Algernon

Swinburne. The semi-derelict medieval castle had been restored and transformed into a romantic fairytale palace in the Gothic revival style beloved of Victorians. One can imagine Christina finding its "enchanted and limitless repose", as the artist William Bell Scott described it, conducive to writing dreamy poetry. It is not hard to envisage her gazing out of a draughty, turreted bedroom on to the ice-hard puddles below, hearing the wind sighing across the Ayrshire farmlands, and picking up her pen.

Into this familiar winter setting she introduces a God who breaks all bonds of time and space, whom heaven cannot hold nor earth sustain, but who makes do with a stable and is happy to accept the simplest worship of the human heart. It is a delicate working of the Christmas theme, restrained by the poise of its poetry on the cliff-edge of sentimentality. In the last verse, the impotence felt by an educated woman in Victorian Britain becomes a symbol of everyone's helplessness, turning both into a rather poignant celebration of the deepest meaning of Christmas.

Even sung to the eager scrape of my daughter's violin at a Christmas recital for gratefully hard-of-hearing grandparents, this hymn has something special.

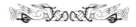

23. WHEN I SURVEY THE WONDROUS CROSS

When I survey the wondrous cross
On which the Prince of Glory died,
My richest gain I count but loss,
And pour contempt on all my pride.

Forbid it, Lord, that I should boast
Save in the death of Christ, my God;
All the vain things that charm me most,
I sacrifice them to his blood.

See, from his head, his hands, his feet,
Sorrow and love flow mingled down;
Did e'er such love and sorrow meet,
Or thorns compose so rich a crown?

His dying crimson, like a robe,
Spreads o'er his body on the tree;
Then am I dead to all the globe,
And all the globe is dead to me.

Were the whole realm of nature mine,
That were an offering far too small;
Love so amazing, so divine,
Demands my soul, my life, my all.

WORDS: Isaac Watts (1674–1748)
MUSIC: "Rockingham", adapted by Edward Miller (1731–1807) from
the melody "Tunbridge" in *A Second Supplement to Psalmody in
Miniature* (c. 1780). Also "Morte Christe" by Emrys Jones.

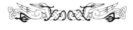

Reflections

The contemporary song-writer Graham Kendrick put his finger on the source of the power of this hymn. "It is all about wonder", he said, "wonder at the seemingly mad extremes of divine love that chooses a crucifixion to atone for evil and conquer death."

No hymn captures so brilliantly and so movingly the timeless paradoxes of what happened on that cross. Here we have an instrument of torture which is also in some extraordinary sense "wondrous", the entire realm of nature constituting too small an offering in the face of such a sacrifice, the richest gain counting for nothing at all, a love being demonstrated which demands nothing less than everything. Familiarity can shrivel these complex ideas into platitudes; in Isaac Watts' hands they are reworked with deceptively simple freshness, yet with a scope which gives the hymn truly epic grandeur.

This offer of "my soul, my life, my all" instigated something of a sea-change in church worship. As a young man preparing to be a Dissenting minister among congregations who thought it frivolous to sing anything but psalms in church services, it took courage for Isaac Watts to produce hymns which allowed the singer to address God directly, and personally. But the trend caught on, and he wrote nearly 600 of them in the end, many of them among the most loved in the canon. This is surely the finest.

I heard it sung recently by the Caernarvon Male Voice Choir to the glorious tune "Morte Christe", which I had never encountered before. The blend of harmonies was spine-tinglingly beautiful, soaring to such a moving climax with the words,

> *Love so amazing, so divine,*
> *demands my soul, my life, my all –*

that there was barely a breath in Bangor Cathedral as the last note died.

On Easter Sunday, when the painted boiled eggs have been ceremonially rolled down the lane behind our house and prizes dispensed for both the furthest travelled and the most inventive (last year awarded to the eldest son, who strapped his egg to a set of wheels), we usually set off for church. It is good to find Isaac Watts there, inviting us to raise our eyes for a moment to something else. Minds crammed with trivia turn to survey a dying Prince. It is another wondrous paradox of Easter.

The ruined town of Balliacrach on the Isle of Mull, where my forebears the McKechnies lived, for a while in the nineteenth century; photograph by Andy Hall from A Sense of Belonging to Scotland, published by Mercat Press.

Lochan-na h-Achlaise, Rannoch Moor, photo courtesy of Derek Prescott.

St Martin cross, a ninth century free-standing cross on the Abbey grounds, Iona, courtesy of Anja Grosse-Uhlmann.

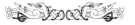

24. WHO CAN SOUND THE DEPTHS OF SORROW

Who can sound the depths of sorrow
in the Father heart of God,
for the children we've rejected,
for the lives so deeply scarred?
And each light that we've extinguished
has brought darkness to our land:
upon the nation, upon the nation
have mercy, Lord.

We have scorned the truth you gave us,
we have bowed to other lords,
We have sacrificed the children
on the altars of our gods.
O let truth again shine on us,
let your holy fear descend:
upon the nation, upon the nation
have mercy, Lord!

Who can sound the depths of mercy
in the Father heart of God?
For there is a Man of sorrows
who for sinners shed his blood.
He can heal the wounds of nations,
He can wash the guilty clean:
because of Jesus, because of Jesus,
have mercy, Lord!

WORDS AND MUSIC: Graham Kendrick (b. 1950)

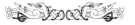

❧ *Reflections* ❧

A Roman Catholic colleague of mine, a television journalist in his twenties, complains that he spent his entire churchgoing youth serving what he calls "a twenty-year sentence to death by Kumbaya".

"Throughout the nineteen seventies and eighties churches were awash with hymns consisting of candy-floss lyrics and sugar-water settings", he said, adding that Catholics seem at last to be rediscovering their musical heritage and no longer feel it necessary to play Simon and Garfunkel's "Bridge Over Troubled Water" during communion.

It is a relief to discover that my own failure to be inspired by many of the contemporary hymns around is neither unique to one religious tradition nor merely a feature of grumpy middle age. I am all for worshipping in an idiom which rings true to modern life, but not if it means eviscerating the challenging truths that the songs are supposed to be communicating.

However, Graham Kendrick composes hymns with a skill and serious-ness of tone which suggest that his admiration of the art of Isaac Watts has paid dividends. In "Who can sound the depths of sorrow" he dares to speak as prophet, calling the nation to repentance. He wrote it with abortion in mind, although a less literal interpretation of the scarred young lives is also valid. He says he tried to capture "an attitude of humble identification as opposed to self-righteous condemnation". Certainly its triumph is in keeping a steady focus on tough mercy and "holy fear" rather than easy emotionalism, and on the strength of the writing:

> *We have scorned the truth you gave us,*
> *we have bowed to other lords,*
> *We have sacrificed the children*
> *on the altars of our gods.*

The Iona Community hymn-writer, John Bell, has described Graham Kendrick as "one of too few writers in the Western world today who allows the sadness at the dark side in our lives to be articulated in a song". He is right. Like Bell himself, his is a genuinely modern voice, articulating concerns and emotions you rarely hear in the hymns of past centuries. He allows a hymn to be angry; he urges social as well as personal penitence. Kendrick deserves a place in the line of hymn-poets of the last thousand and more years whose songs have helped us to see, to feel and to remember. The image of Christ's crucifixion in another song of his, "The Servant King" –

> *hands that flung stars into space*
> *to cruel nails surrendered –*

is among the most arresting in any hymn.

I'm sure Kendrick's hymns will be remembered when the candy-floss is long blown away.

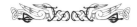

25. GLORIOUS THINGS OF THEE ARE SPOKEN

Glorious things of thee are spoken,
Sion, city of our God;
He whose word cannot be broken
Formed thee for his own abode.
On the Rock of Ages founded,
What can shake thy sure repose?
With salvations's walls surrounded,
Thou may'st smile at all thy foes.

See, the streams of living waters,
Springing from eternal love,
Well supply thy sons and daughters,
And all fear of want remove:
Who can faint, while such a river
Ever flows their thirst to assuage:
Grace, which like the Lord the giver,
Never fails from age to age?

Saviour, if of Sion's city
I, through grace, a member am,
Let the world deride or pity,
I will glory in thy name:
Fading is the worldling's pleasure,
All his boasted pomp and show;
Solid joys and lasting treasure
None but Sion's children know.

WORDS: John Newton (1725–1807)
MUSIC: Franz Joseph Haydn (1732–1809)

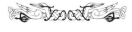

❧ *Reflections* ❧

Everything John Newton did was to such excess and accompanied by such drama that the summary of his life reads like a Hollywood film proposal.

We can imagine the pitch. This fellow starts out as a coarse and rascally eighteenth-century sailor. Falls desperately in love and deserts ship. Is press-ganged back on board in chains, flogged, demoted and goes berserk. Escapes off the west coast of Africa, where he works on a plantation, is mistreated and begins to live like a savage. Letter from his father encourages return to England. Storm on voyage home nearly wrecks ship and prompts him to reassess life and values. Rediscovers religion of his childhood and becomes well-behaved sea-captain on slave-trading line. But something is missing – he finds eighteenth-century religion unsatisfying and longs for a faith he can surrender to fully. Through "amazing grace" (title of one of his future hymns and, doubtless, of proposed bio-pic) he is converted to passionate faith in Christ. After a struggle to be ordained, he finally becomes minister at Olney and rushes about preaching, teaching and indefatigably writing hymns, some of which are pretty dreadful and a few brilliant. He flames with refocused energy.

"Get Russell Crowe on board immediately!" I hear the film mogul barking.

What a life. The energy which pulsated through John Newton's personality, hurling him into wild excesses as a sailor, flinging him into love and out of ships, and later catapulting him with burning heart into the Christian ministry, is there in his hymns too. Especially this one.

Maybe I am imagining it, but I have always detected a hint of rumbustiousness in "Glorious things of thee are spoken", a whiff of the pugnacious sailor of old. Here he is, secure in the fortress of believers, smiling with what is surely defiance at his foes, cheerfully challenging the world to "deride or pity" and engaging in some deft derision himself of the "worldling" and his pleasures. It is a combative hymn from a man who has done it all and seen it all and concluded that the lasting treasure belongs to those who glory in one thing alone: "thy name." His theme is grace, but, true to the man, it is dynamic grace.

This is a choppier ride than the serene cruises we take with some hymn writers. The setting is less sublime and the river scene a little hackneyed. But the captain is exhilarating company.

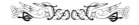

26. ALL IN THE APRIL EVENING

All in the April evening
April airs were abroad.
The sheep with their little lambs
Passed me by on the road.

The sheep with their little lambs
Passed me by on the road.
All in the April evening
I thought on the lamb of God.

The lambs were weary and crying
With a weak human cry.
I thought on the lamb of God
Going meekly to die.

Up in the blue, blue mountains,
Dewy pastures are sweet.
Rest for the little bodies,
Rest for the little feet.

But for the Lamb of God
Up on the hilltop green
Only a cross of shame,
Two stark crosses between.

All in the April evening,
April airs were abroad.
I saw the sheep with their lambs
And thought of the Lamb of God.

WORDS: Katharine Tynan (1861–1931)
MUSIC: Hugh Roberton (1874–1952)

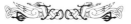

࿇࿇ *Reflections* ࿇࿇

I know this is a choral classic rather than strictly a hymn, but it is so fabulously evocative of one night of the year that I have to include it. Perversely, this night is neither an Easter evening, nor even (you might be grateful to learn) during the season when frisking lambs normally require rest for their little feet. Rather it is midwinter Hogmanay, the night when the Scots traditionally let their hair down and the New Year in.

Little has changed about our Hogmanay celebrations as far back as I can remember, except that my mother's ginger wine was long ago usurped by stronger beverages and her twin sister can no longer be bothered slipping out of the house after midnight and returning to ring the bell and pass herself off as a tall, dark stranger bearing a piece of coal. Music remains at the heart of the evening, with Scots folk songs sung lustily around the piano and then, at a suitably advanced stage of the evening, party pieces performed – everything from Flanders and Swann and a wildly off-key "Sisters", to a recent year's Australian medley by a somewhat dazed quartet of antipodean visitors, followed by an actor friend doing his *Hamlet*-in-three-minutes monologue.

But the most keenly awaited moment of the evening is always the singing of "All in the April evening", the song popularised by the renowned Glasgow Orpheus Choir in their heyday in the first half of the last century. The words were written by the Dublin-born poet and novelist Katharine Tynan, who is less well known these days for her prolific literary efforts than for having received a proposal of marriage from Ireland's poetic giant, W. B. Yeats. In setting Tynan's "Sheep and Lambs" to a musical arrangement of his own, the Orpheus' founder and conductor Hugh Roberton did what talented composers have been doing down the centuries: he transformed a sentimental poem into a hymn of considerable power. In their youth my mother and her two sisters, Anna and Harriet, used to go and hear Roberton's choir in Glasgow, and they loved this piece so much that they taught themselves the three-part harmony. When my father, not a man renowned for his religious fervour, first heard it, he was so entranced that it quickly became a staple of family get-togethers.

Their voices are a mite shaky now and the postures stooped, but when these three sisters begin to sing in harmony on New Year's Eve, there is no lovelier sound in all the world. Glasses are put down, chatter stilled and suddenly the Lamb of God is there in the room in the midst of our rowdy Hogmanay celebrations.

It has never felt incongruous to switch from a singularly vigorous "Waltzing Matilda" to the lyrical sadness of "All in an April evening". The verses may look twee on the page, but the combination of melody, word-picture and pacing is so perfect that it transports every one of us, in the way that the best hymns always do, to another place.

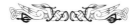

27. GUIDE ME, O THOU GREAT JEHOVAH

Guide me, O thou great Jehovah,
Pilgrim through this barren land;
I am weak, but thou art mighty;
Hold me with thy powerful hand:
Bread of heaven,
Feed me till my want is o'er.

Open now the crystal fountain,
Whence the healing stream doth flow;
Let the fire and cloudy pillar
Lead me all my journey through:
Strong deliverer,
Be thou still my strength and shield.

When I tread the verge of Jordan,
Bid my anxious fears subside;
Death of death, and hell's destruction,
Land me safe on Canaan's side:
Songs of praises
I will ever give to thee.

WORDS: William Williams (1717–1791)
TRANSLATION: Peter Williams (1722–1796) and others
MUSIC: "Cwm Rhondda" by John Hughes (1873–1932)

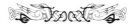

Reflections

It is nearly 20 years since I first presented *Songs of Praise*. Much as I enjoy my normal journalistic diet of live news and gladiatorial current affairs, the programme inspired by Britain's tenacious affection for hymns has provided an entirely different kind of satisfaction.

It has enabled me to escape the politically charged hot air of the studio and sit in the homes of ordinary (although invariably they turn out to be extraordinary) men and women who have taken the worst and the best that life can deal, wrestled with excruciating moral dilemmas, faced death, made sacrifices, beaten fear, found joy and learned things of inestimable value to pass on in life. And with their stories have come the hymns, sung in settings as various and eclectic as the programme itself, from village chapel to the loftiest cathedral, from street, fairground, aircraft hangar and sports stadium to mountain, boat and even (see page 67) a train.

"Guide me, O thou great Jehovah" is rarely far from a *Songs of Praise* running order. It is a big, exuberant hymn, with a satisfyingly fitting nod to the programme's name in the finale. It is also gloriously, wondrously Welsh. To hear a male voice choir from that nation raise the roof and puncture the clouds themselves with the harmonies of "Cwm Rhondda" is bliss of a high order indeed.

As a hymn-writer William Williams was the Isaac Watts, or perhaps the Charles Wesley, of Wales. He preached the length and breadth of the country on horseback, just as the Wesley brothers were doing in England, spreading the same dynamically revived gospel with the aid of about 800 hymns which he wrote himself in his native tongue. Most of these remain untranslated, but in 1771 the unrelated Peter Williams produced the first version of "Guide me, O thou great Jehovah" in English. Much later, at the beginning of the twentieth century, the addition of the "Cwm Rhondda" tune, composed for a Pontypridd singing festival, turned this thoughtfully symbolic depiction of spiritual pilgrimage into a pan-British favourite.

The Welsh bass-baritone Bryn Terfel explained to me once that for his countrymen hymns were not something to be trapped in churches. Native speakers like himself, born, bred and in love with every last stone in the rugged north, sang them all the time in their own tongue, as naturally as breathing. I wish more were available in translation. Hearing him and his compatriots drifting in and out of one hymn after another, as comfortable with the Welsh words as the delicious harmonies, I realised how much the rest of us were missing.

Thank goodness, at least, for "Bread of Heaven".

28. BURNS GRACE

O thou who kindly dost provide
For every earthly creature's need,
We bless thee, God of nature wide,
For goodness known in word and deed;
And if it please thee, heavenly guide,
May nothing worse be ever sent;
But whether granted or denied,
Lord, bless our souls with deep content.

As much as nature can provide,
Much more we carelessly demand,
And heedless of the world in want
We hesitate to lend a hand;
O gen'rous maker of us all,
Whose joy it is to foster good,
Teach us that openness of heart
Which shares and values daily food.

WORDS: Robert Burns (1759–1796), adapted by John Bell
TUNE: "Ye banks and braes", Scottish traditional air

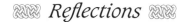 Reflections

I first heard this hymn when presenting *Songs of Praise* from the village of Alloway in Ayrshire, where Scotland's national poet Robert Burns was born in a two-roomed cottage in 1759. The congregation there introduced us to the Burns Grace, which had been written by the bard himself (the first verse, at any rate) and adapted by the hymn-writer and "Songs of Praise" conductor John Bell. It was sung to the tune of "Ye banks and braes o' bonnie Doune", the river which wanders through Alloway just a stone's throw from the church.

Burns is better known for his coruscating indictments of clerical hypocrisy than his prayers, and when it comes to his "Graces before Meat", most of us will prefer the simple Scots one –

> *Some hae meat and canna eat,*
> *And some wad eat that want it;*
> *But we hae meat and we can eat,*
> *Sae let the Lord be thankit –*

to the more self-consciously poetic and anglicised grace on which this hymn is based:

> *O Thou, who kindly does provide*
> *For ev'ry creature's want!*
> *We bless Thee, God of Nature wide,*
> *For all Thy goodness lent.*
> *And if it please Thee, heavenly Guide,*
> *May never worse be sent;*
> *But, whether granted or denied,*
> *Lord, bless us with content!*

Still, it is a pleasure to find any lines of Robert Burns being sung by modern congregations – as well as being an irony which Burns, who suffered the full rigours of kirk discipline over his affairs of heart and loins, would no doubt appreciate. His songs and poems are more often heard at whisky-soaked Burns Suppers than in church. All the more credit, then, to John Bell for demonstrating that, as far as Rabbie is concerned, a church is not merely a building redolent of draconian eighteenth-century humiliation at the penance stool, but a place where a little of his work and the humane spirit behind it can comfortably reside.

In an attempt to marry the eighteenth century with the twenty-first, Bell's second verse adds a modern slant to the familiar Burnsian theme of the dignity of all men, with a plea for wisdom when it comes to sharing the world's resources. It also extends the idea of a grace from a private muttering of thanks for a meal to a public prayer of global scope. It is an ambitious undertaking, gracefully executed.

29. THE LORD'S MY SHEPHERD

(PSALM 23)

The Lord's my shepherd, I'll not want.
He makes me down to lie
in pastures green; he leadeth me
the quiet waters by.

My soul he doth restore again,
and me to walk doth make
within the paths of righteousness,
ev'n for his own name's sake.

Yea, though I walk in death's dark vale,
yet will I fear none ill;
for thou art with me, and thy rod
and staff me comfort still.

My table thou hast furnished
in presence of my foes;
my head thou dost with oil anoint,
and my cup overflows.

Goodness and mercy all my life
shall surely follow me;
and in God's house for evermore
my dwelling-place shall be.

WORDS: Scottish Psalter (1650), based on Psalm 23
MUSIC: Several tunes, including "Crimond", ascribed to
Jessie S. Irvine (1836–1887)

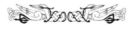

❧ *Reflections* ❧

How could I not include "The Lord's my shepherd"? The one metrical psalm which I know by heart has followed me, in its own words, "all my life": from dimly remembered school services to Sunday mornings within the cool stone walls of Baldernock kirk, from the joyous opening blast at my wedding to the harrowing service at Dunblane cathedral after the shooting of the children, from tremulous singing at funerals to mighty *Songs of Praise* choirs in full harmonious flight.

Its chief author was David, "sweet psalmist of Israel", but the miracle of the version preserved for us in the Scottish Psalter of 1650, in which no line is awry, no word superfluous and the whole comprises an elegantly flowing narrative, is that it was composed by committee. As the writer Andrew Barr has pointed out, the composition was a long and complicated process, involving the revision of an earlier text of 1643. Despite civil war and ecclesiastical turmoil, psalm texts were carried backwards and forwards between Scotland and England (united at the beginning of the century under King James VI and I), while being distributed to different poets whose revisions were then sent on to members of the various courts of the Presbyterian church. Eight different authors were involved in revising Psalm 23; an earlier translation by King James himself, who had tried his hand at versifying a number of psalms, is said to linger in the line "shall surely follow me".

Somehow or other this tortuous process was touched by genius. With pellucid fluency the authors managed to capture the psalmist's vision of provision and protection in this life, the soul's quiet restoration and a dwelling-place with God for ever after. The image of the Lord as a shepherd, combining strength with comfort, is beautifully sustained, while the two strongest lines of all

Yea, though I walk in death's dark vale,
yet will I fear none ill

have helped carry more people through death to whatever lies beyond than the anonymous poet, or poets, who crafted them could have dreamed. Who has ever put it better?

Jessie Irvine, daughter of the minister of the little Aberdeenshire village of Crimond, is usually credited with having composed the best loved of all the accompanying tunes. Her "Crimond" is still my favourite, but a number of other musical settings also work well – not least the wistful air "O rowan tree", which accompanied the psalm when it was so poignantly sung at Dunblane cathedral in 1996.

It is a measure of the strength of the poetry that, rarely among hymns, the tune barely matters. It is the words which generations of people have hugged to themselves until their dying day.

30. LORD, YOU HAVE COME TO THE SEA-SHORE

Lord, you have come to the sea-shore,
neither searching for the rich nor the wise,
desiring only that I should follow.

O, Lord, with your eyes set upon me,
gently smiling, you have spoken my name.
All I longed for I have found by the water;
at your side, I will seek other shores.

Lord, see my goods, my possessions;
in my boat you find no power, no wealth.
Will you accept, then, my nets and labour?

Lord, take my hands and direct them.
Help me spend myself in seeking the lost,
returning love for the love you gave me.

Lord, as I drift on the waters,
be the resting place of my restless heart,
my life's companion, my friend and refuge.

WORDS: "Pescador de Hombres" by Cesáreo Gabarain, 1978
TRANSLATION: Robert C. Trupia, 1987
MUSIC: Joseph Abell

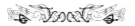

ᘓᘓᘓ *Reflections* ᘓᘓᘓ

Early in the nineteen-eighties, in the soft blue air of a Roman spring, I accompanied Glasgow's then archbishop, Thomas Winning, to the Vatican, where he had an appointment with the Pope to discuss John Paul II's forthcoming visit to Scotland. It was a newspaper assignment which gave me a chance to get to know and like the man who would later become Scotland's down-to-earth, shoot-from-the-lip cardinal. When he died suddenly in 2001, the BBC asked me to the lead the television commentary at his funeral.

The music that day was as rich as the visual spectacle, which began with hundreds of priests processing into the cathedral in their billowing white robes to join the solemn drama of the funeral mass. But nothing in the beautiful sonorities of the service deflected us for long from Tom Winning the man, the priest who loved his people and eschewed as much of the pomp associated with his elevated role as he possibly could.

One hymn in particular gave us a vivid flash of his personality and the faith which had motivated him, a jaunty song, gorgeously harmonised, which began:

> *Lord, you have come to the sea-shore*
> *neither searching for the rich nor the wise.*

It had been Cardinal Winning's favourite. Prince of the Church he may have been, but as someone who had spent all the money collected for a planned renovation of St Andrew's Cathedral on the deprived children of Glasgow instead, he had been able to sing with more justification than many:

> *Lord, see my goods, my possessions;*
> *in my boat you find no power, no wealth.*

Thomas Joseph Cardinal Winning

"Pescador de Hombres" was written by the Spaniard Cesáreo Gabarain. I'm told it was brought to Britain in various translations by priests who trained at the Scots College in Spain, where this sweet meditation on Christ's invitation to the disciples to follow him has caught the imagination and become a popular anthem. It has a catchy melody and a narrative which is as meaningful a metaphor to the children who sing it gustily in school as it was to the Cardinal himself, who found there a prayer which inspired him to the very end of his life:

> *Lord, as I drift on the waters,*
> *be the resting place of my restless heart,*
> *my life's companion, my friend and refuge.*

Some consider the song fluffy, and I can see their point. But whatever the unique alchemy which takes word, arrangement, context and the way you happen to be feeling when you hear it, and transforms it into gold, it happened to this hymn for me. I suppose we just have to face the fact that one person's candy-floss can be another's cloud of glory.

31. DEAR LORD AND FATHER OF MANKIND

Dear Lord and Father of mankind
Forgive our foolish ways;
Reclothe us in our rightful mind;
In purer lives thy service find,
In deeper reverence praise.

In simple trust like theirs who heard
Beside the Syrian sea,
The gracious calling of the Lord,
Let us, like them, without a word
Rise up and follow thee.

O Sabbath rest by Galilee!
O calm of hills above,
Where Jesus knelt to share with thee
The silence of eternity,
Interpreted by love!

With that deep hush subduing all
Our words and works that drown
The tender whisper of thy call,
As noiseless let thy blessing fall
As fell thy manna down.

Drop thy still dews of quietness,
Till all our strivings cease;
Take from our souls the strain and stress,
And let our ordered lives confess
The beauty of thy peace.

Breathe through the heats of our desire
Thy coolness and thy balm;
Let sense be dumb, let flesh retire;
Speak through the earthquake, wind, and fire,
O still small voice of calm!

WORDS: John Greenleaf Whittier (1807–1892)
MUSIC: "Repton" by Hubert Parry (1848–1918)

⚂⚃ *Reflections* ⚂⚃

I am generally suspicious of hymns which set spiritual and physical experience in opposition, as if God were not the maker of all flesh as well as all souls. In fact, you would think that weddings, where "Dear Lord and Father of mankind" is particularly popular, would be the last sort of occasion to bid sense be dumb and flesh retire. But this hymn works for other reasons. The broadcaster Huw Edwards has said he chose it for his own wedding because it is about "celebration, praise, lifelong faith and God's guidance". And that is true. It is a hymn which helps us all to seek out the "still small voice of calm" in the midst of life's relentless hurry – and does it beautifully.

Its scene is the same Galilean idyll that Cesáreo Gabarain captures in "Lord, you have come to the sea-shore". But this is more passive and penitential, less concerned with rolling up the sleeves and casting out the nets than with kneeling at Jesus's side by the lake to bask in a kind of holy hush. Even eternity here is silent. It is no surprise to discover that the hymn was written by a Quaker.

John Greenleaf Whittier was born in 1807 into the Quaker community at Haverhill in Massachusetts, New England. He became a journalist and threw himself into a campaign against slavery, but his hobby – and his solace amid the hurly-burly of public affairs – was to write poetry. In 1872 he penned what he called a "hymn-poem" intriguingly entitled "The Brewing of Soma", which boasted 17 verses. Verse 12 is the start of what became "Dear Lord and Father of mankind", a hymn which is quintessentially Quaker in its evocation of stillness and silence in communion with God.

My own life is as rushed and febrile as anyone's in this hectic age. Although live TV broadcasts, bickering school runs and journalistic deadlines may not constitute an "earthquake, wind and fire" exactly, they certainly feel like it sometimes. Amid it all, I badly need those dews of quietness and voice of calm. If all my strivings do not cease at the singing of this hymn, they are at least put into perspective for a while.

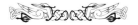

32. ABIDE WITH ME

Abide with me: fast falls the eventide;
The darkness deepens; Lord, with me abide;
When other helpers fail, and comforts flee,
Help of the helpless, O abide with me.

Swift to its close ebbs out life's little day;
Earth's joys grow dim, its glories pass away;
Change and decay in all around I see;
O thou who changest not, abide with me.

I need thy presence every passing hour;
What but thy grace can foil the tempter's power?
Who like thyself my guide and stay can be?
Through cloud and sunshine, O abide with me.

I fear no foe with thee at hand to bless;
Ills have no weight, and tears no bitterness.
Where is death's sting; where, grave, thy victory?
I triumph still, if thou abide with me.

Hold thou thy cross before my closing eyes;
Shine through the gloom, and point me to the skies·
Heaven's morning breaks, and earth's vain shadows flee;
In life, in death, O Lord, abide with me.

WORDS: Henry Francis Lyte (1793–1847)
MUSIC: "Eventide" by William Henry Monk (1823–1889)

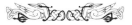

⚜ *Reflections* ⚜

If we were to learn that Henry Lyte had written "Abide with me" after a bracing game of golf, with years of rude health ahead of him, would we appreciate it in the same way? I only ask because the picture which has been handed down of the dying Devonshire vicar, sitting down to pen his final elegy after tea on the last Sunday he preached at Brixham, has cast such a compelling spell over the hymn itself that it is hard to be rid of it. Without it, might the hymn seem a mite overwrought?

When you know that the writer was gravely ill with consumption and would soon be breathing his last on a trip to the south of France, the images of deepening darkness, dimming joys and closing eyes are rather poignant. Shorn of that empathetic context, they can seem sentimental. But no matter. The success of a hymn ultimately lies in how much you like singing it, and I love the slightly Gothic drama of "Abide with me", with the shining Cross being borne aloft before the drooping eyes, and then heaven breaking in like the sun of the morning to banish the shadows. As is obvious from earlier hymns like "Praise, my soul, the King of heaven" (see page 73), Henry Lyte was no mean poet.

As a matter of fact it is not certain that he was actually dying when he wrote the hymn. Born in 1793 in Kelso in the Scottish borders, Lyte was an Anglican priest in Ireland before he moved to the English fishing village of Brixham. As a young clergyman in his first Irish charge, he is said to have sat with a neighbouring priest who was near death and read for him the account in Luke's gospel of two travellers meeting the risen Jesus on the road to Emmaus. One school of thought holds that he composed "Abide with me", with its opening allusion to the words of those wayfarers – "Abide with us: for it is toward evening and the day is far spent" – there and then.

Whatever the truth of its composition, the hymn acknowledges a reality we all have to face and does so with much grace. Running through it is man's age-old argument with death, realised here in as dramatic a poetic sequence as any hymn-writer has attempted. It moves from the despairing "Help of the helpless, O abide with me" to a rhetorical defiance of the grave which, in turn, rather endearingly falters a little in the last verse, leaving us with a final image at once vulnerable and hopcful.

The accompanying tune, which the London organist William Monk apparently composed in ten minutes flat, is wonderful, as football fans have known ever since "Abide with me" became the opener to the 1927 English F.A. Cup Final. A bizarre choice it may have been, but those fans had taste.

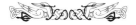

33. O LOVE THAT WILT NOT LET ME GO

O Love that wilt not let me go,
I rest my weary soul in thee;
I give thee back the life I owe,
That in thine ocean depths its flow
May richer, fuller be.

O Light that followest all my way,
I yield my flickering torch to thee;
My heart restores its borrowed ray,
That in thy sunshine's blaze its day
May brighter, fairer be.

O Joy that seekest me through pain,
I cannot close my heart to thee;
I trace the rainbow through the rain,
And feel the promise is not vain
That morn shall tearless be.

O Cross that liftest up my head,
I dare not ask to fly from thee:
I lay in dust life's glory dead,
And from the ground there blossoms red
Life that shall endless be.

WORDS: George Matheson (1842–1906)
MUSIC: "St Margaret" by A. L. Peace (1844–1912)

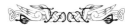

🞘🞘 *Reflections* 🞘🞘

Every time he spots a struggling rainbow, my husband can be relied on to regale the company with a snatch of "O Love that wilt not let me go". He considers it the most beautiful of all hymns. Reluctant as I am to bolster this man's conviction that he is invariably right about everything, I have to concede he has a point here.

It was written by Glasgow-born George Matheson, a Church of Scotland minister who, despite losing his sight at the age of eighteen, was known as a brilliant scholar and one of the country's finest preachers. He composed it on a summer's evening in 1881 at his hillside manse at Innellan, an Argyllshire village "doon the watter" from Glasgow on the Firth of Clyde. By that time of day the steamers would have collected the last of the daytrippers from the pier. Gulls would still be complaining shrilly over the waves far below the manse, as Matheson picked up his pen to pour his heartbreak into a hymn.

It used to be thought that he had been jilted by a girl he hoped to marry, but the truth is that Matheson was careful to ensure that no one ever knew exactly what had provoked him into writing this most intense and emotional of hymns. "Something had happened, known only to myself, which caused me the most severe mental distress," he wrote later. "The hymn was the fruit of that suffering." All we know is that his sister, who had been his housekeeper, companion and in every sense his eyes – she had even learned Latin, Greek and Hebrew to help with his studies – was getting married that day. Unable to attend the celebrations in Glasgow, he was at home alone. Possibly he was feeling very alone indeed.

Matheson described "O Love that wilt not let me go" as a hymn "wrung out of my heart", which he composed in three minutes and neither corrected nor retouched, almost as if someone were dictating it. I can find nothing rushed about the thoughtful structure and intricate metaphors, but the hymn does have a strong sense of naked emotion. Perhaps the reason people like it so much today is that, unlike other hymns of the time which to our questioning age can seem over-confident and even brash, Matheson's insights are almost tentative. The best he can say of the rainbow's promise for the morn is that it is "not vain", while Christ is someone he "dares not" ask to fly from. All of which makes his final resolution, the glorious blossoming of a new life amid the ashes of all our hopes and achievements, the more sensationally (in every sense of the word) powerful. With poetry, faith and ineffable melody working together, it does everything you can possibly ask of a hymn:

> *I lay in dust life's glory dead,*
> *And from the ground there blossoms red*
> *Life that shall endless be.*

Norman has instructed me to make sure this one is high on the agenda at his funeral; frankly, I wouldn't dare not to. But then, perhaps, to be practical about things, it will be he who ends up selecting the programme for mine. If so, someone might care to remind him that I, too, would be very happy with "O Love that wilt not let me go".

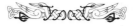

34. BE THOU MY VISION

Be thou my vision, O Lord of my heart;
Naught be all else to me, save that thou art,
Thou my best thought, by day or by night,
Waking or sleeping, thy presence my light.

Be thou my wisdom, thou my true word;
I ever with thee, thou with me, Lord;
Thou my great Father, I thy true son;
Thou in me dwelling, and I with thee one.

Be thou my battle-shield, sword for the fight,
Be thou my dignity, thou my delight.
Thou my soul's shelter, thou my high tower:
Raise thou me heavenward, O Power of my power.

Riches I heed not, nor man's empty praise,
Thou mine inheritance, now and always:
Thou and thou only, first in my heart,
High King of heaven, my treasure thou art.

High King of heaven, after victory won,
May I reach heaven's joys, O bright heaven's Sun!
Heart of my own heart, whatever befall,
Still be my vision, O Ruler of all.

WORDS: Ancient Irish, c. 8th century
TRANSLATION: Mary Byrne (1880–1931)
VERSIFYING: Eleanor Hull (1860–1935)
MUSIC: "Slane", traditional Irish melody

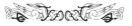

꩜ *Reflections* ꩜

Ah, but this (funeral arrangers, take note) is the hymn I love best of all. Strange in a way, because there is no part of my life thus far to which it uniquely belongs, no season when it is routinely sung, no occasion that has invested it with a special memory. Yet whenever I sing "Be thou my vision", my spirit soars – or at the very least it rises bumpily off the ground and flies for a while. Somehow the essence of a near-perfect hymn is captured here, some indefinable "quidditie", to quote George Herbert, in which word, form and music unite to express the deepest things of the heart in exactly the right way.

I dare say each of us will find this quiddity in all sorts of different places, nudged there by tradition and taste. Perhaps it is no surprise that the hymn which speaks pre-eminently for a fervid Scot with a romantic bent should be plain and strong, passionate and intimate, decidedly ancient and, yes, very Celtic – qualities in a hymn to which I seem always drawn. My imagination leaps to embrace the ardour of the unknown Irish composer, a hermit saint, perhaps, heir of Columba, withdrawing to some wild and remote place to make space for the presence of God.

Two women, both Irish, gave us the hymn in its present form. In 1905 Mary Byrne, an Anglo-Irish scholar, made a prose translation in English of a poem dating from around the eighth century. A few years later Dr Eleanor Hull turned it back into poetry, again keeping close to the original, and published it in 1912 in her *Poem Book of the Gael*. There are minor differences among the versions in use today but, whichever one we sing, we can all be grateful to those translators for rejecting poetic flourishes and ornate syntax and letting my hermit monk, or warrior-priest, or whoever he was, continue to speak in the unadorned but dramatically personal idiom of the Celtic Christian.

It is a hymn which feels ageless. God is my best thought, my light, my wisdom, my dignity, my delight, my father, my power, my soul's shelter, my high king. Even the images of turbulent eighth-century warfare – the battle-shield (or breastplate in some versions), sword and defensive stone tower – reinforce the universal need for soul-shelter. In an age of easy wealth and shallow celebrity, it is good to have a voice from long, long ago reminding us where the real treasure lies and helping us to sing the most timelessly beautiful of all prayers to our Maker:

> *Heart of my own heart, whatever befall,*
> *still be my vision, O ruler of all.*

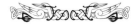

35. THE LORD BLESS THEE AND KEEP THEE

The Lord bless thee and keep thee.
The Lord make his face to shine upon thee
And be gracious unto thee.
The Lord lift up his countenance upon thee
And give thee peace.
Amen.

Numbers 6, 24–26

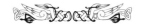

❦ *Reflections* ❦

This is really a blessing rather than a hymn, but I thought I might sneak it in right at the end, since it expresses so well what all my favourite hymn-writers have been on about, from Celtic monk to contemporary scribbler, medieval Pope to American Quaker, including along the centuries poets metaphysical, mystical and pre-Raphaelite, a retired slave-trader, a bunch of Methodists, a shoal of Victorian clergymen, a Spaniard, an Icelander, a German, an Austrian and my own Scottish great-grandfather.

Where are they all taking us but towards the Lord who would bless and keep us? What are they all asking but that somehow, amid the agonies and frustrations and joys and follies, the aspirations and the worries, the interminable sorrows and fleeting moments of ecstasy which have ever made up our lives, God might make his face to shine upon us and be, in that lovely, grave word, "gracious" unto us. Their cry is that he would lift up his countenance upon us and, in life and death alike, give us the commodity which eludes humankind most persistently: peace.

The blessing, taken directly from the Bible, is the one which Aaron and his sons were commanded to pronounce over the people of Israel. I have heard it sung most often after the baptism of infants: if "By cool Siloam's shady rill" didn't have us reaching for a tissue, the slow, steady rise and fall of the notes of "The Lord bless thee and keep thee" certainly did. But this is not just a blessing for a baby. It is an anthem for everyone, all the time. A hymn for life.